DILLON GEORGE

A Moment In Pictures

As a photographer, I strive to create a fusion of fashion and documentary-based work. Having a keen eye for beauty and style guides me in making aesthetically pleasing images while being surrounded by a diverse community allows me to capture the real unscripted moments. Challenging the traditional boundaries between these polar opposite styles opens my work to thought-provoking themes that capture the true essence of my subjects and the world around them. Working with my peers inhabit an authentic experience for both me and the subject to capture their individuality as if the camera wasn't there.

In each of my projects, I go into it with an unrestricted mind and allow my subject to freely reflect themselves through the lens. Whether I'm setting up a fixed environment or stopping in place and snapping the raw reality of what is in front of me, creating something that is emotionally impactful is my goal. My setup often involves strong composition, depth of field, and natural lighting as the full recipe for my final image. Using a variety of mixed media such as paper and stickers used for symbolism adds to my personal style.

My ultimate goal as a photographer is to create a body of work that inspires, educates, and resonates with my audience. Showing authentic stories in my images is what drives my passion to keep creating. Sparking conversation between the masses when they see my work is what is going to challenge people's perspectives and allow my work to live on. I truly believe that a single image can both capture the styled and candid moments in life

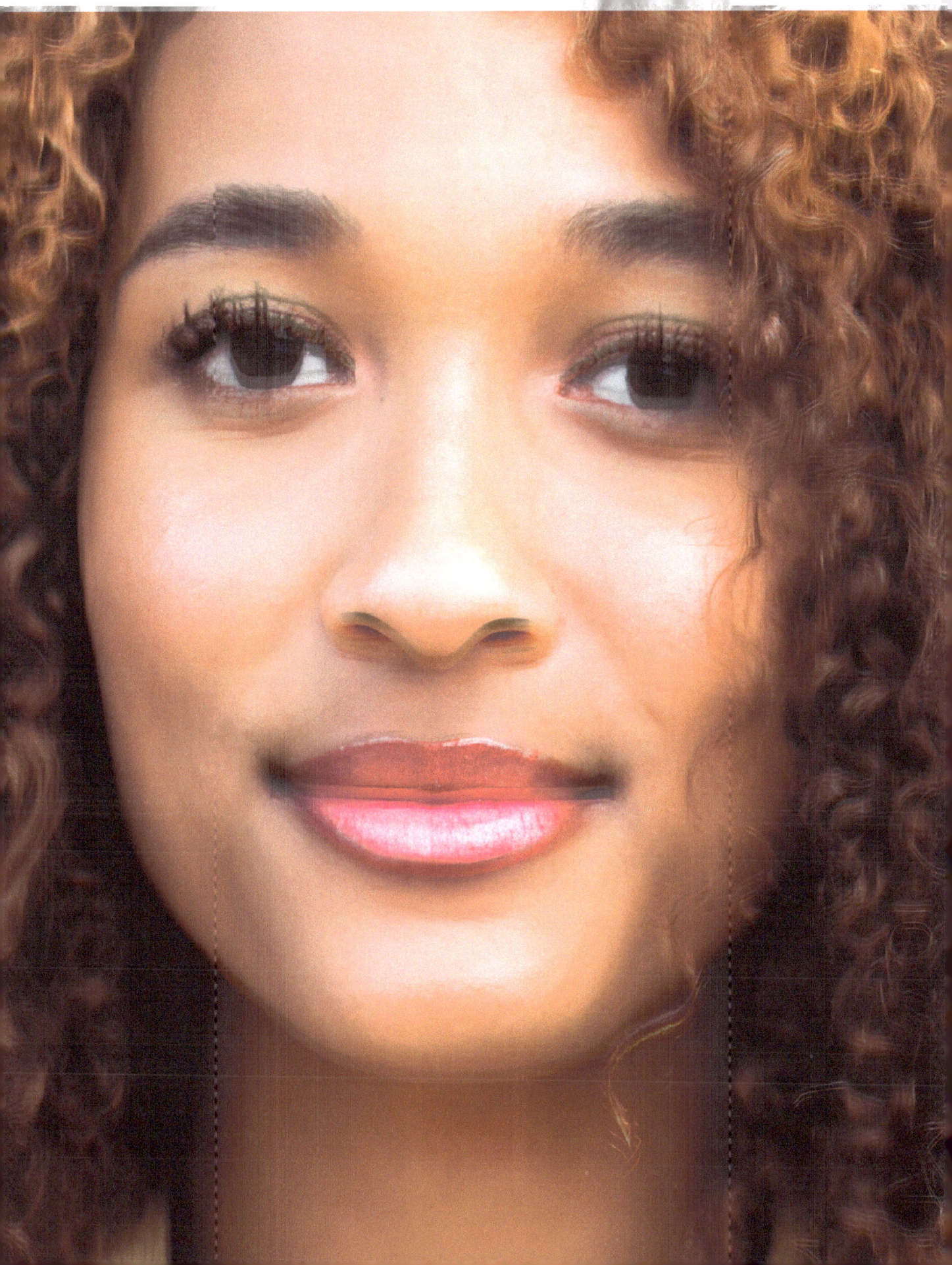

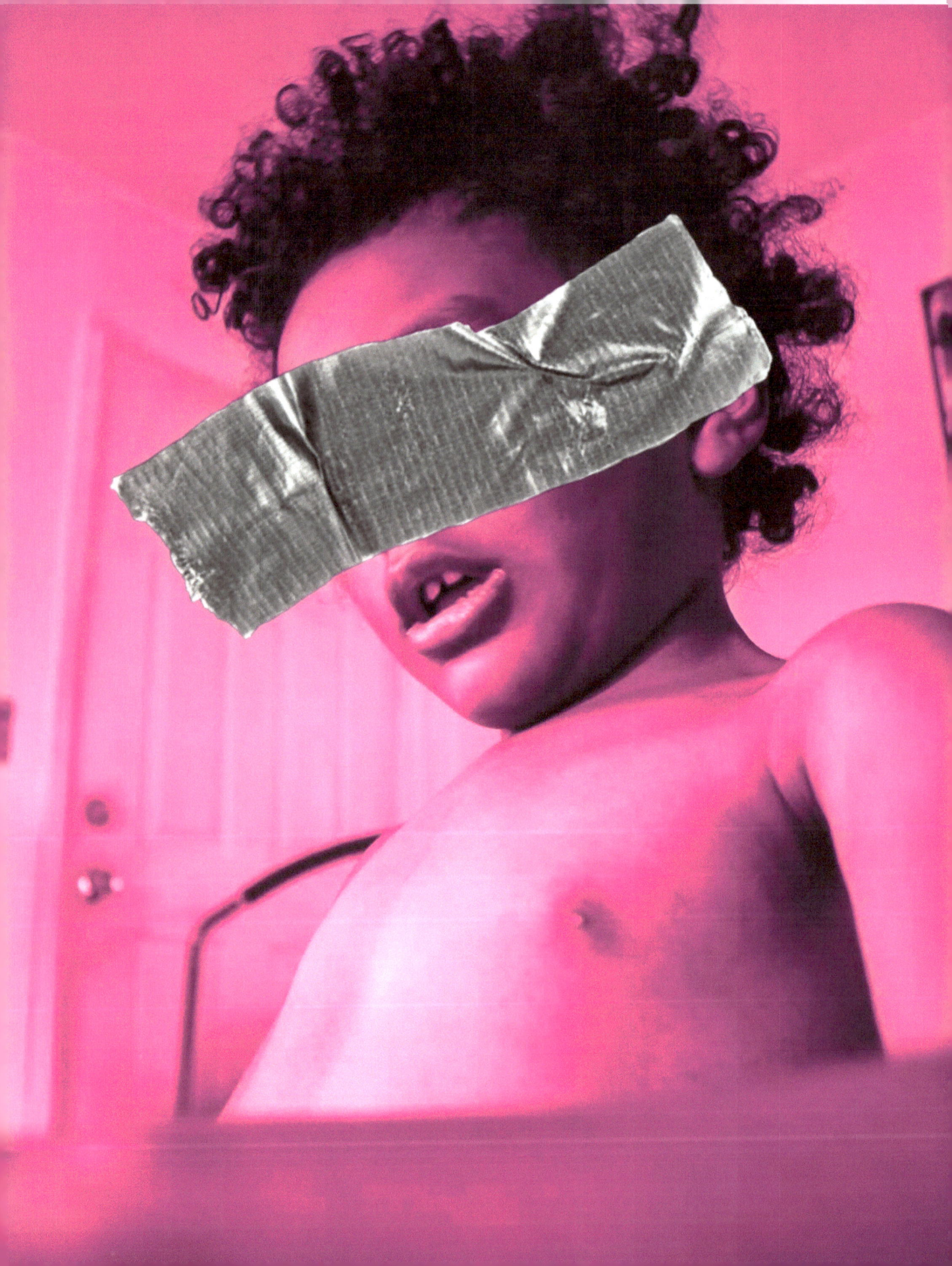

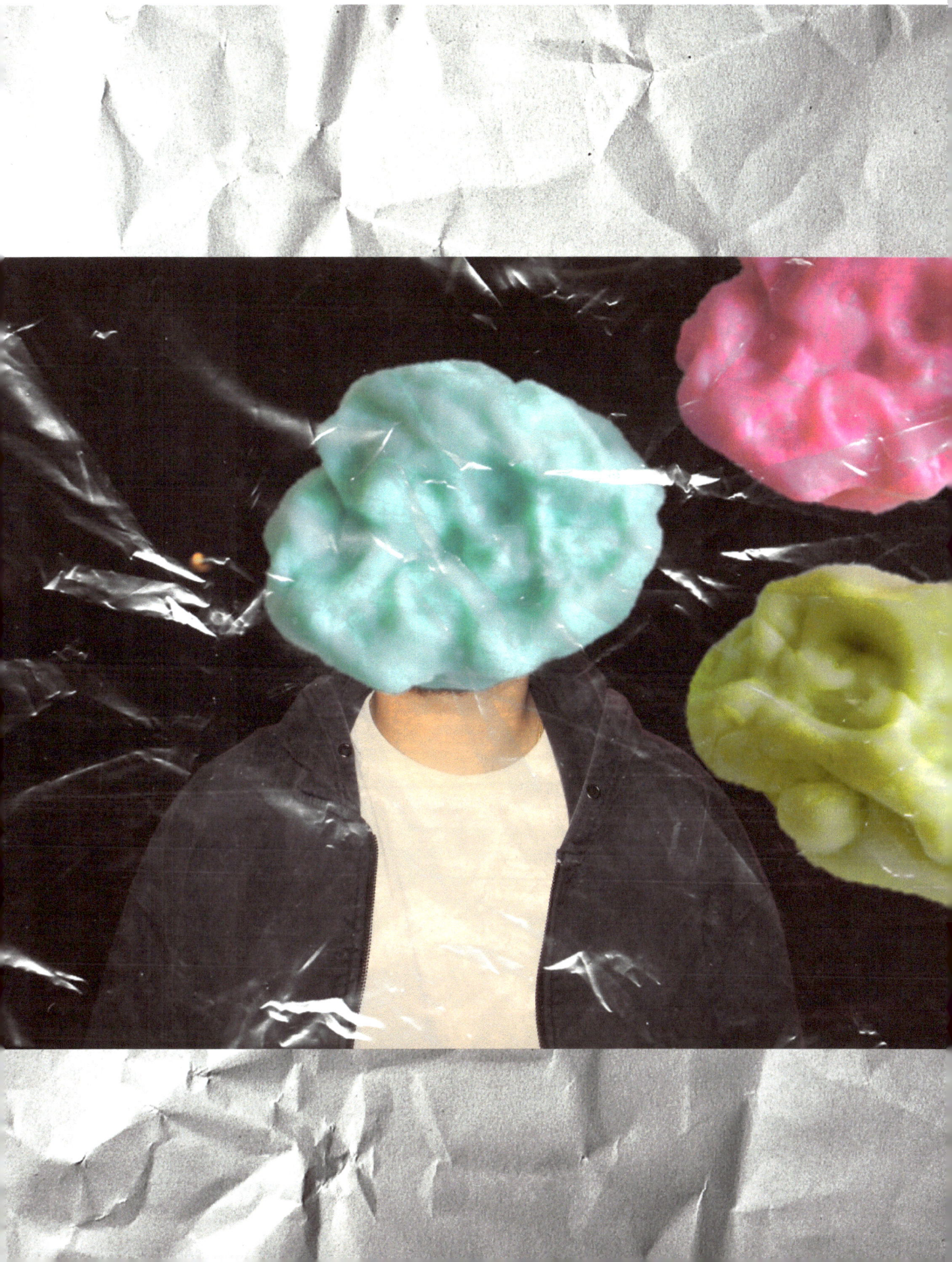

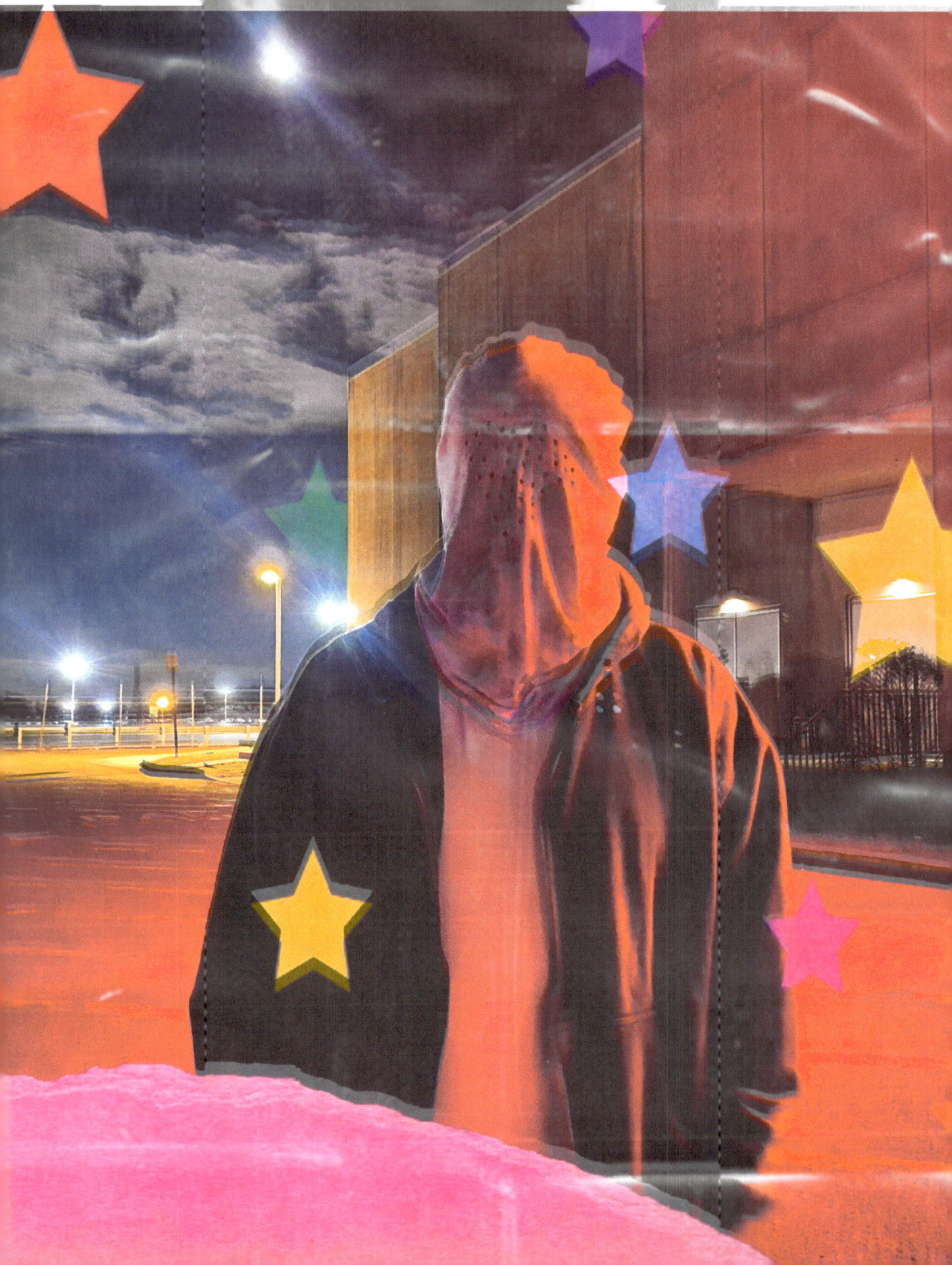

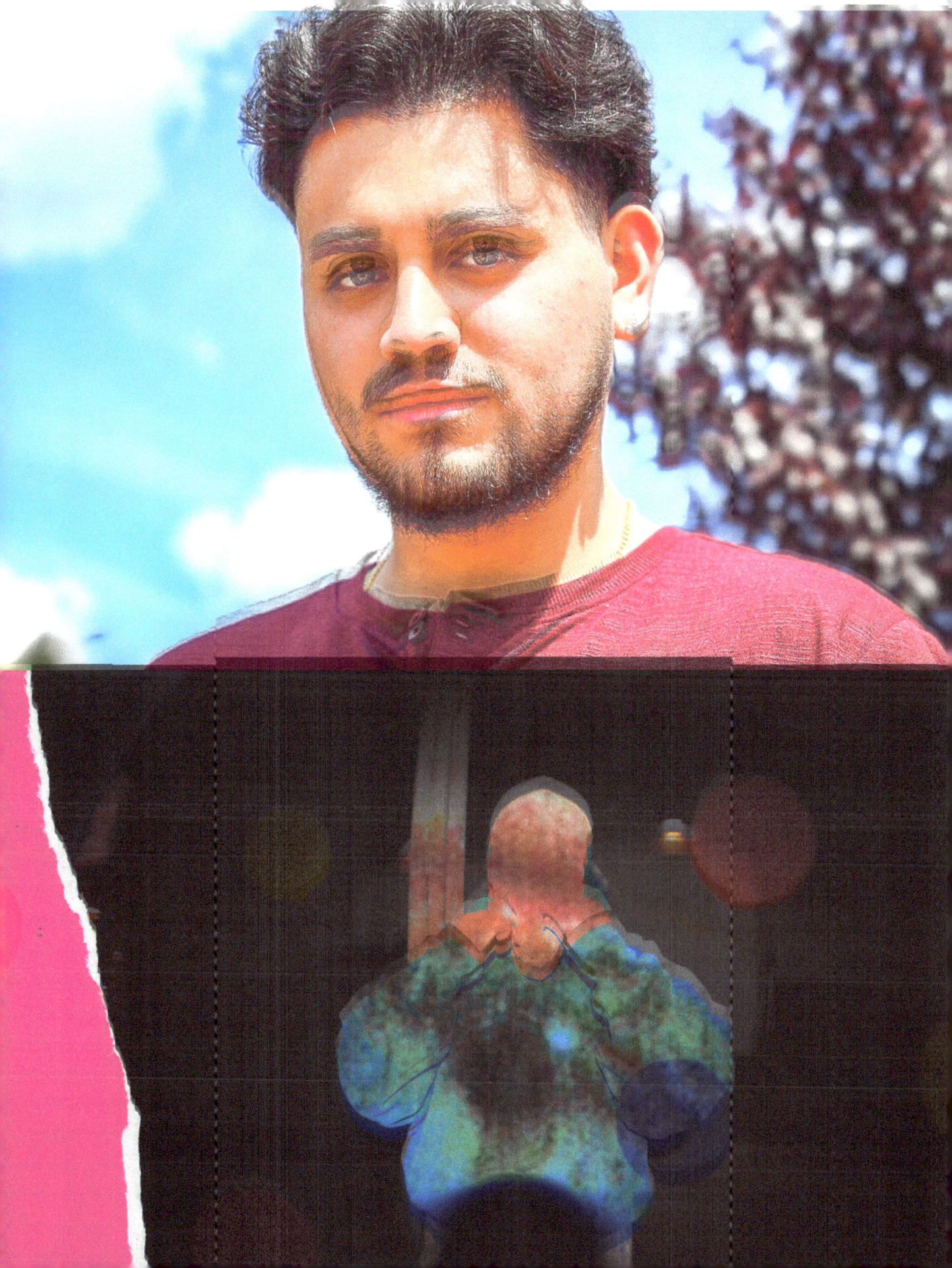

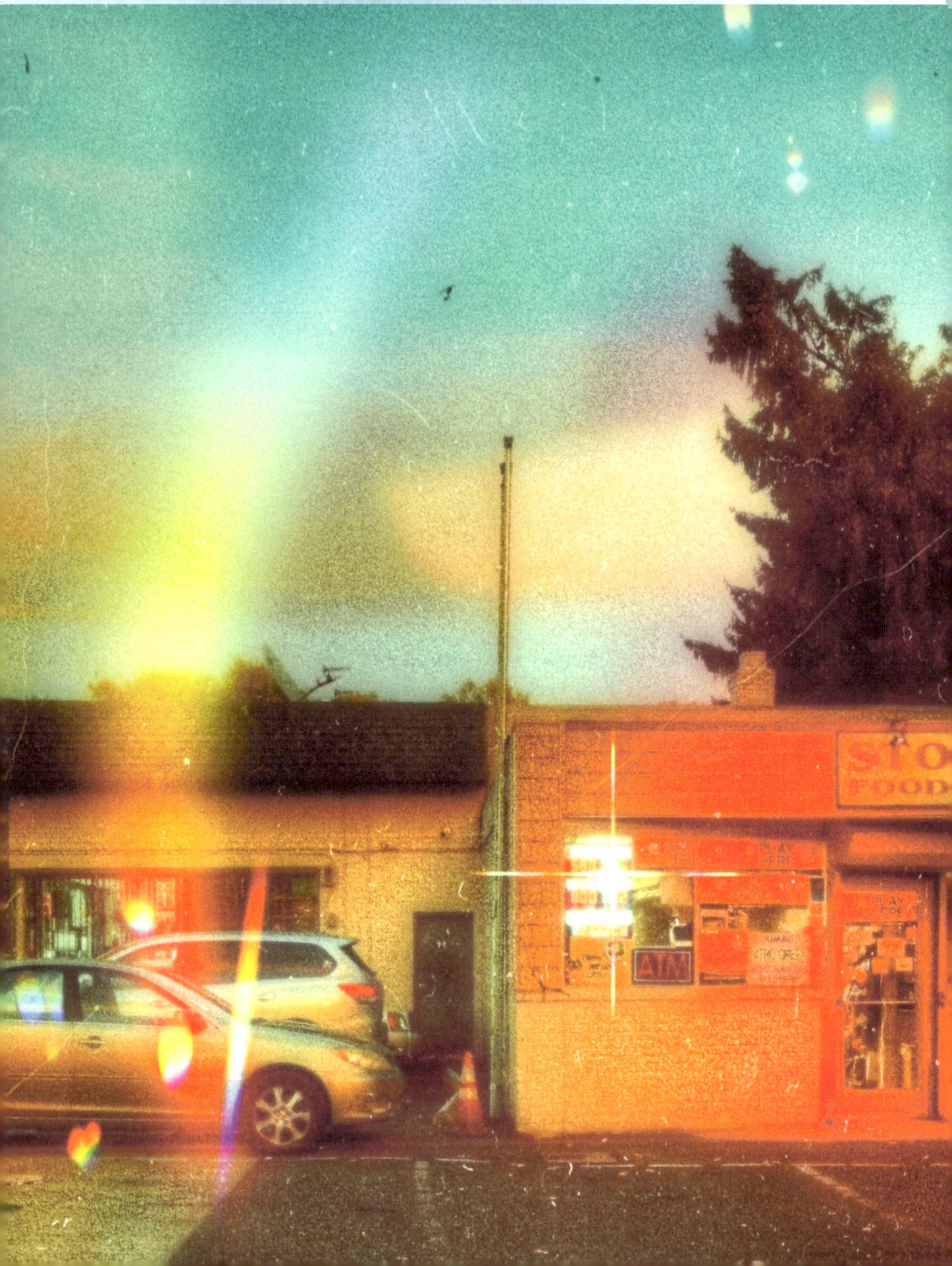

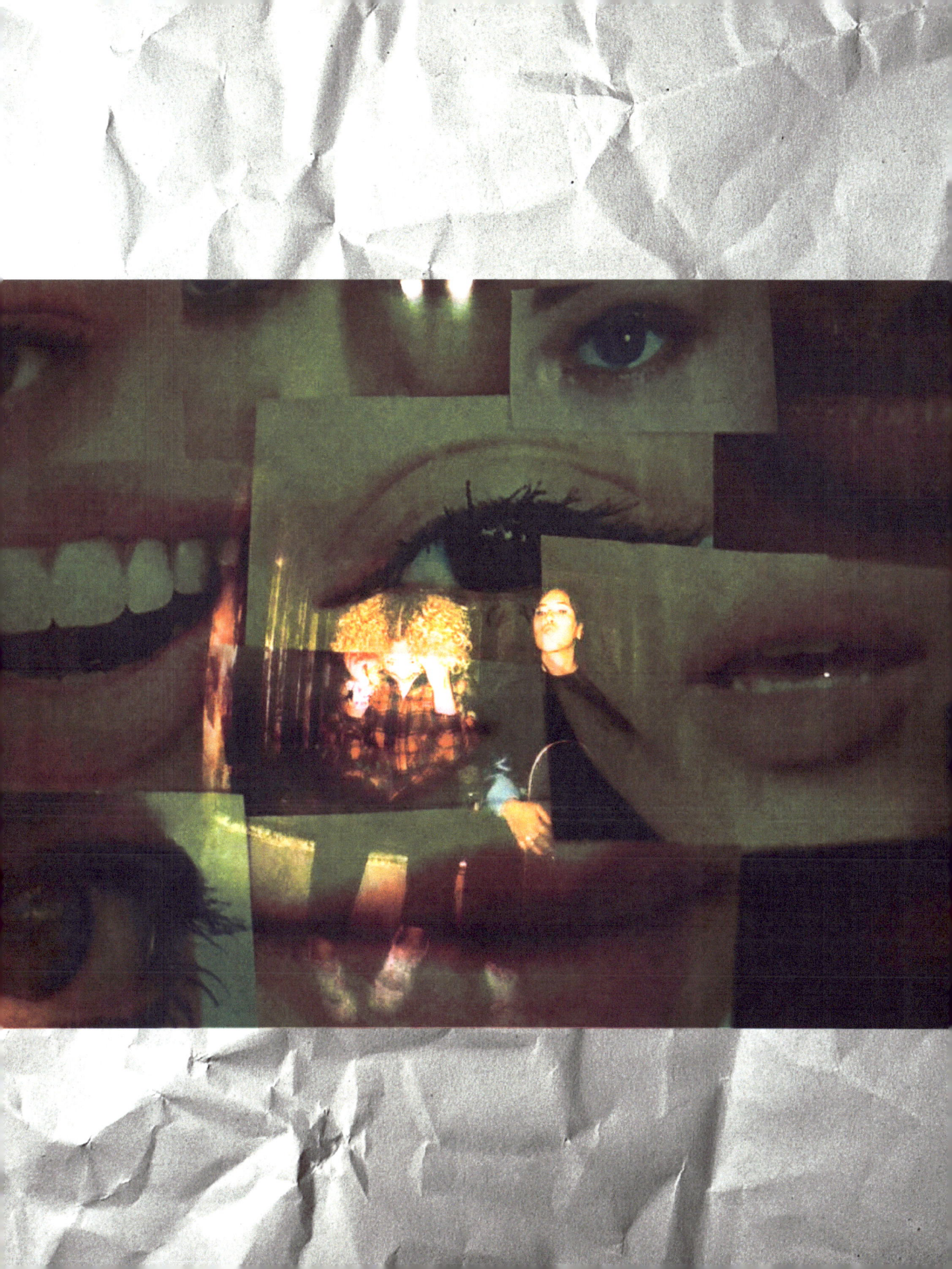

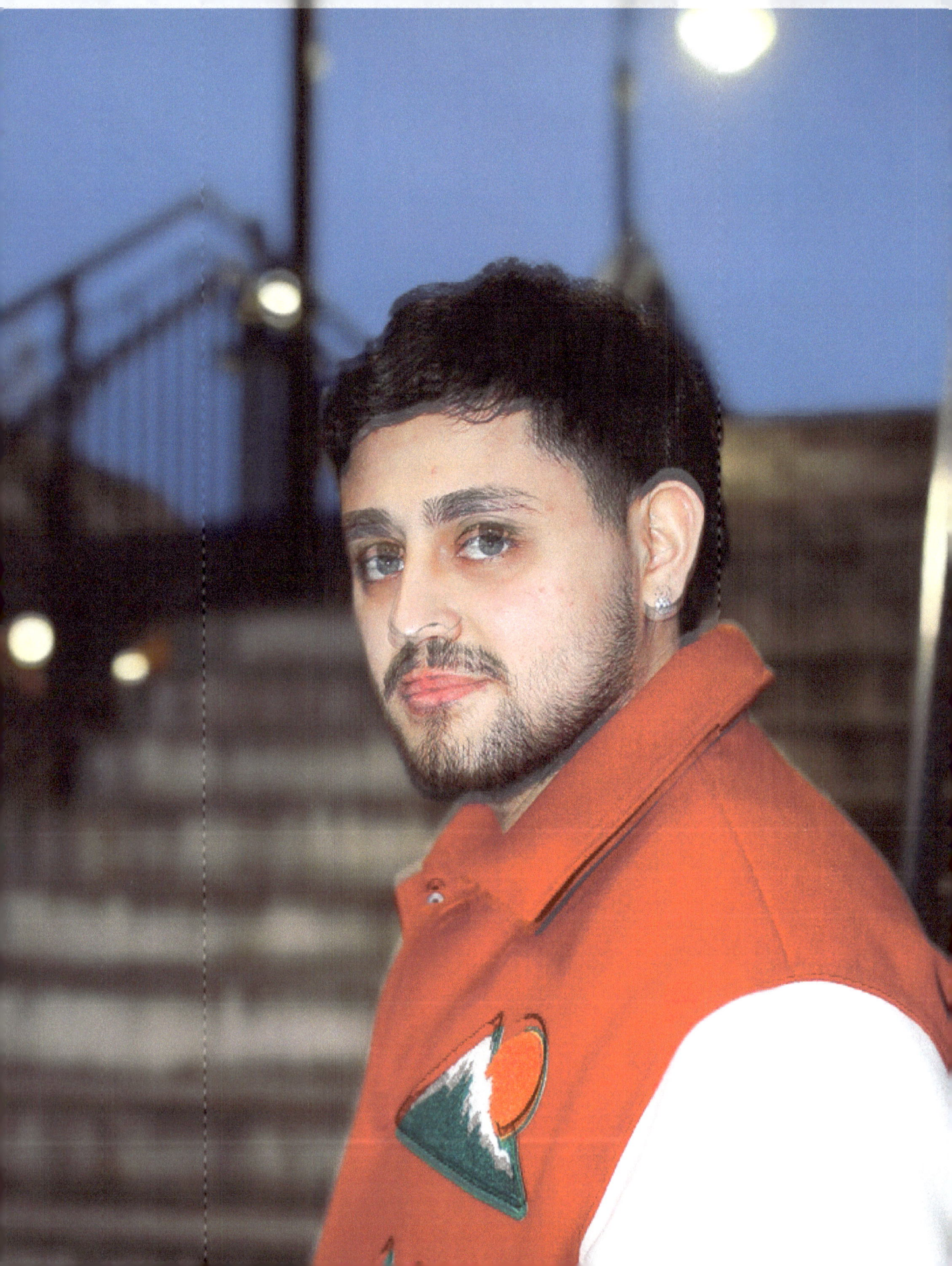

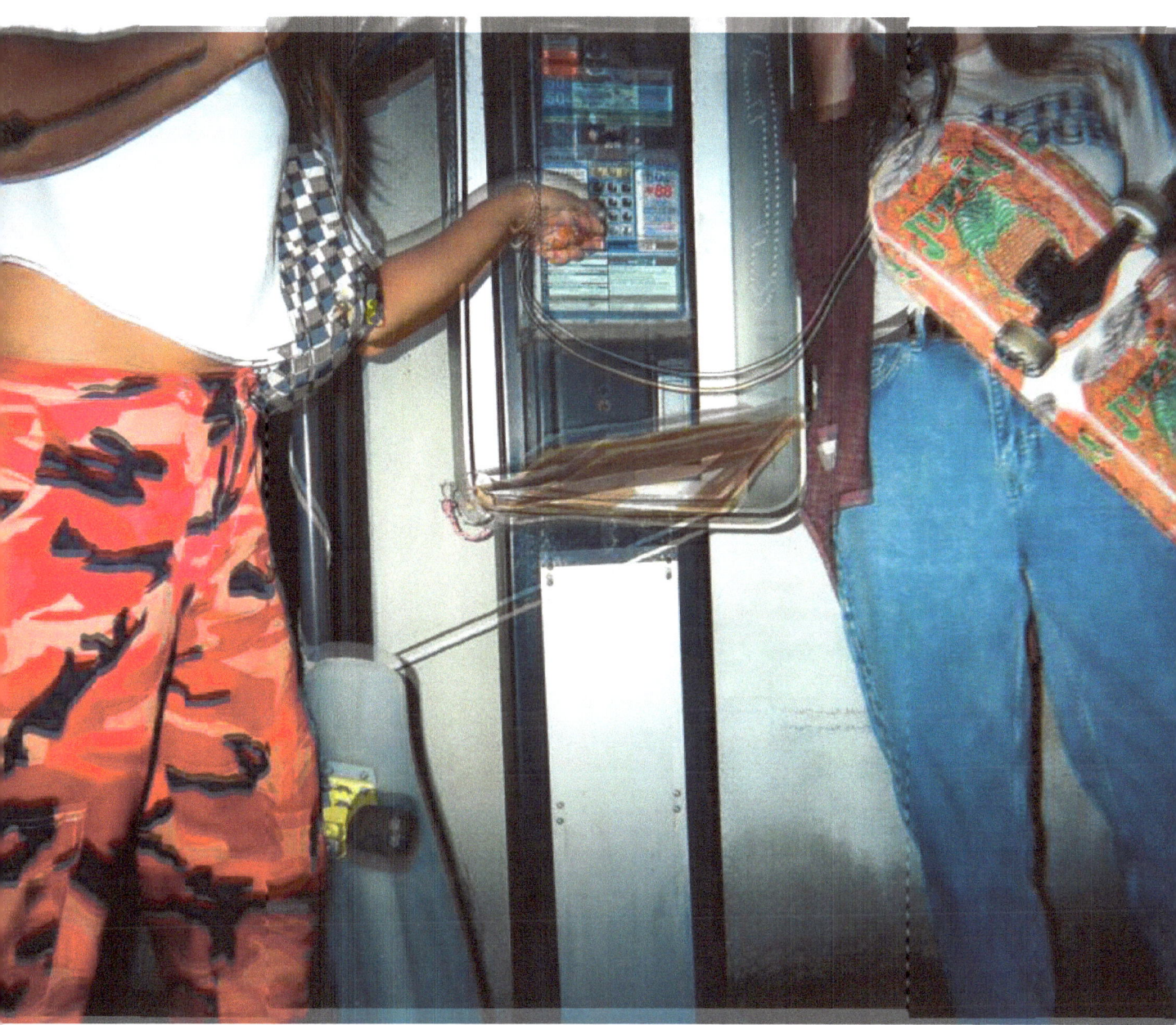

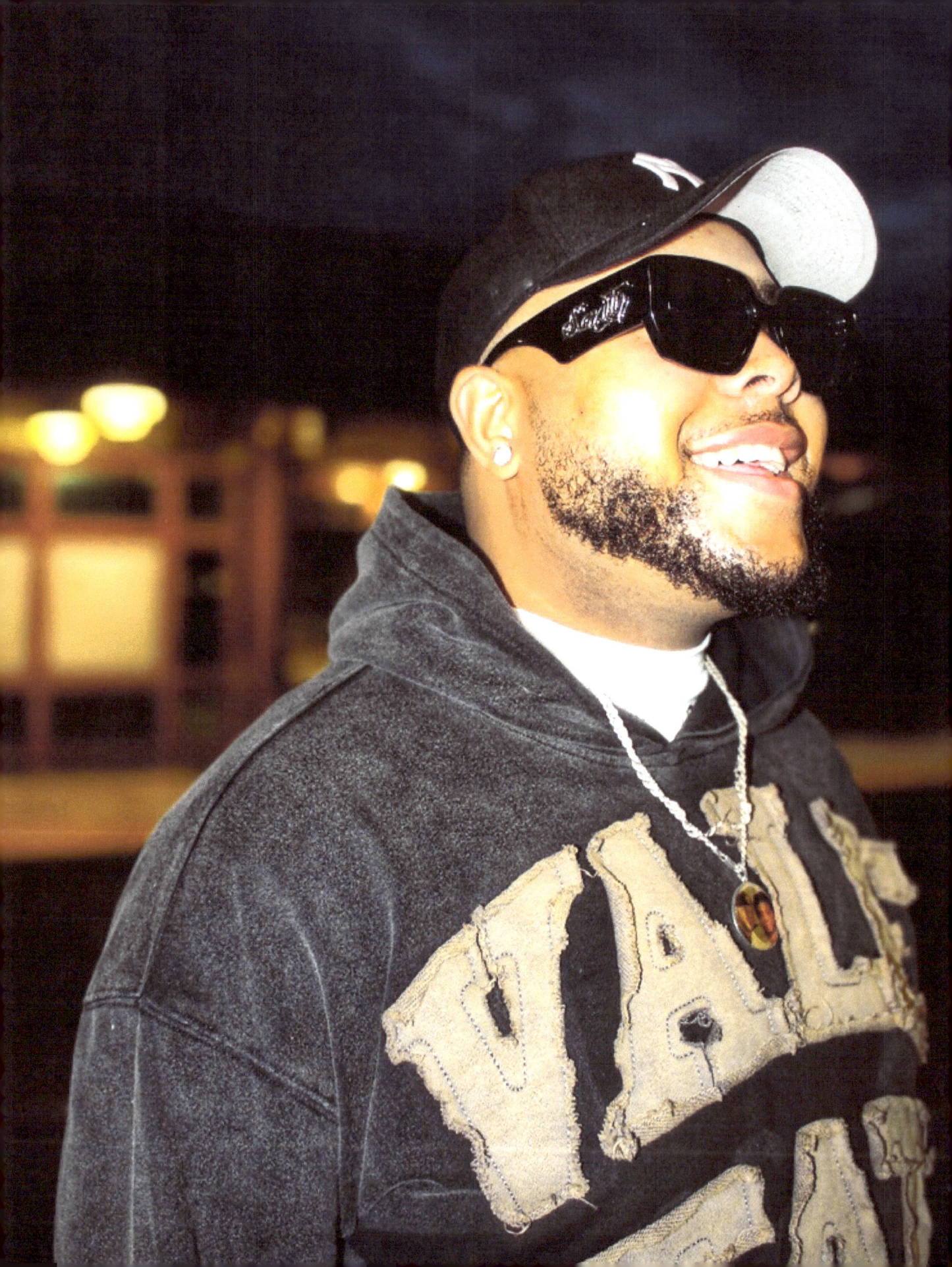

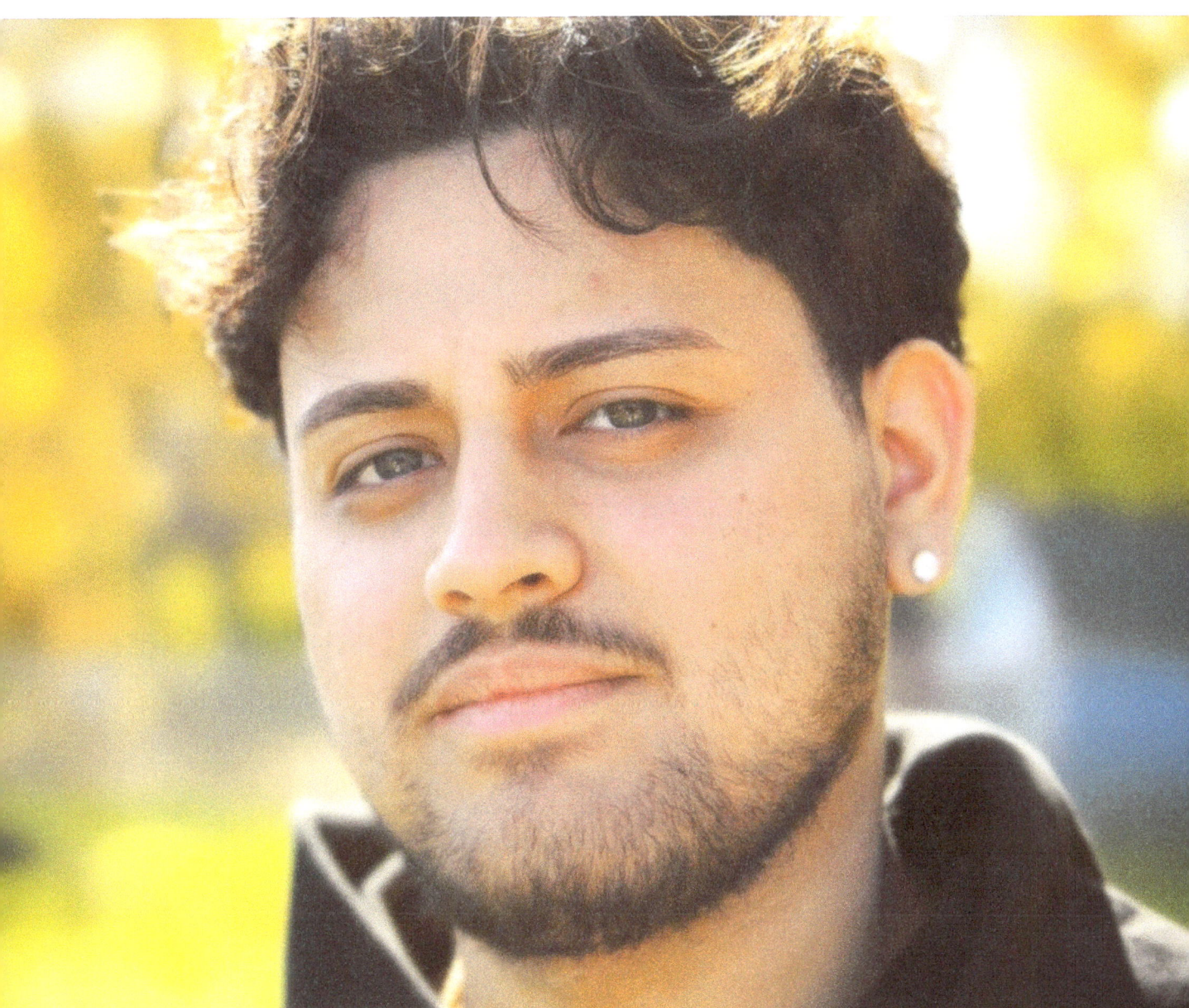

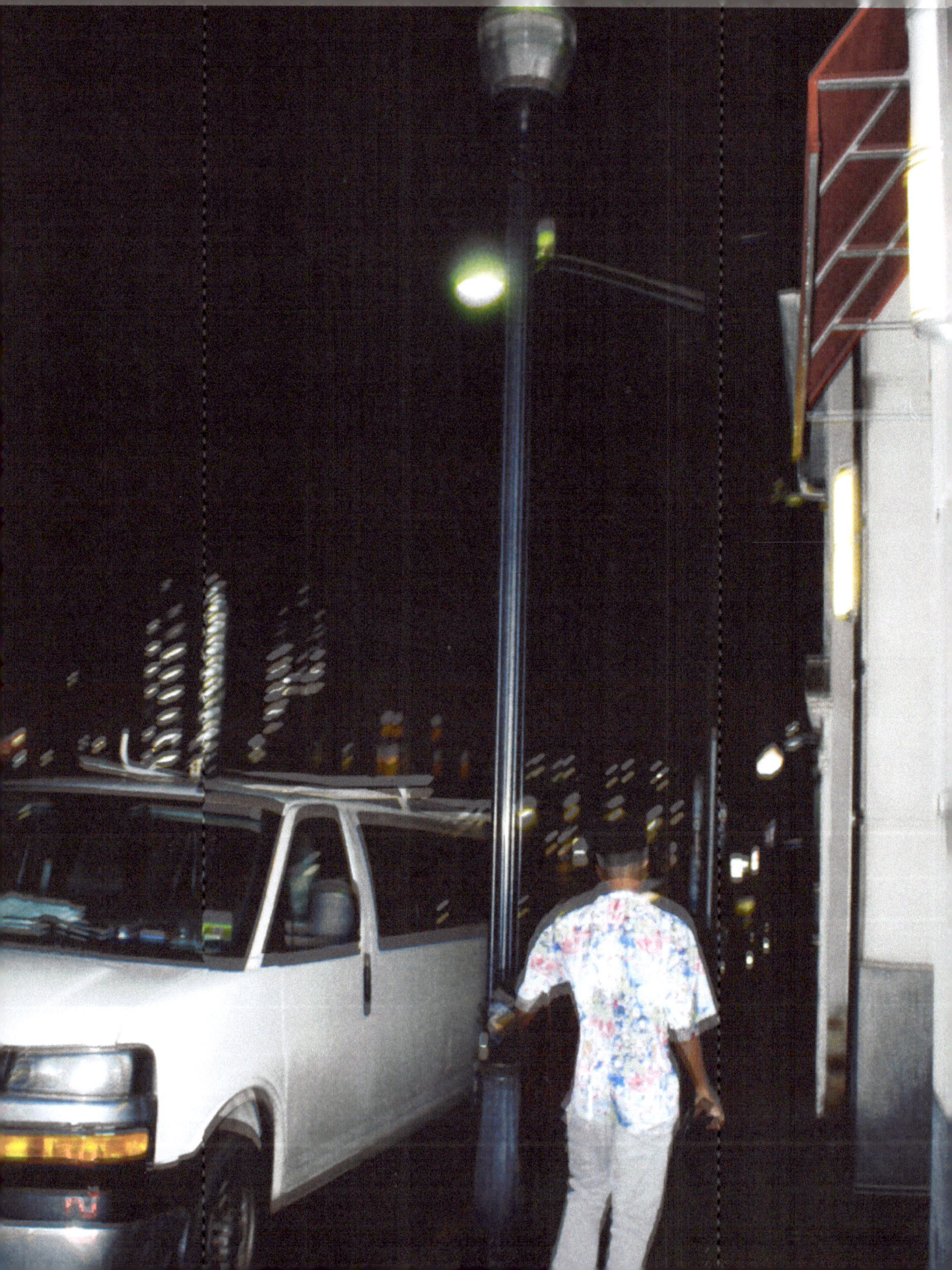

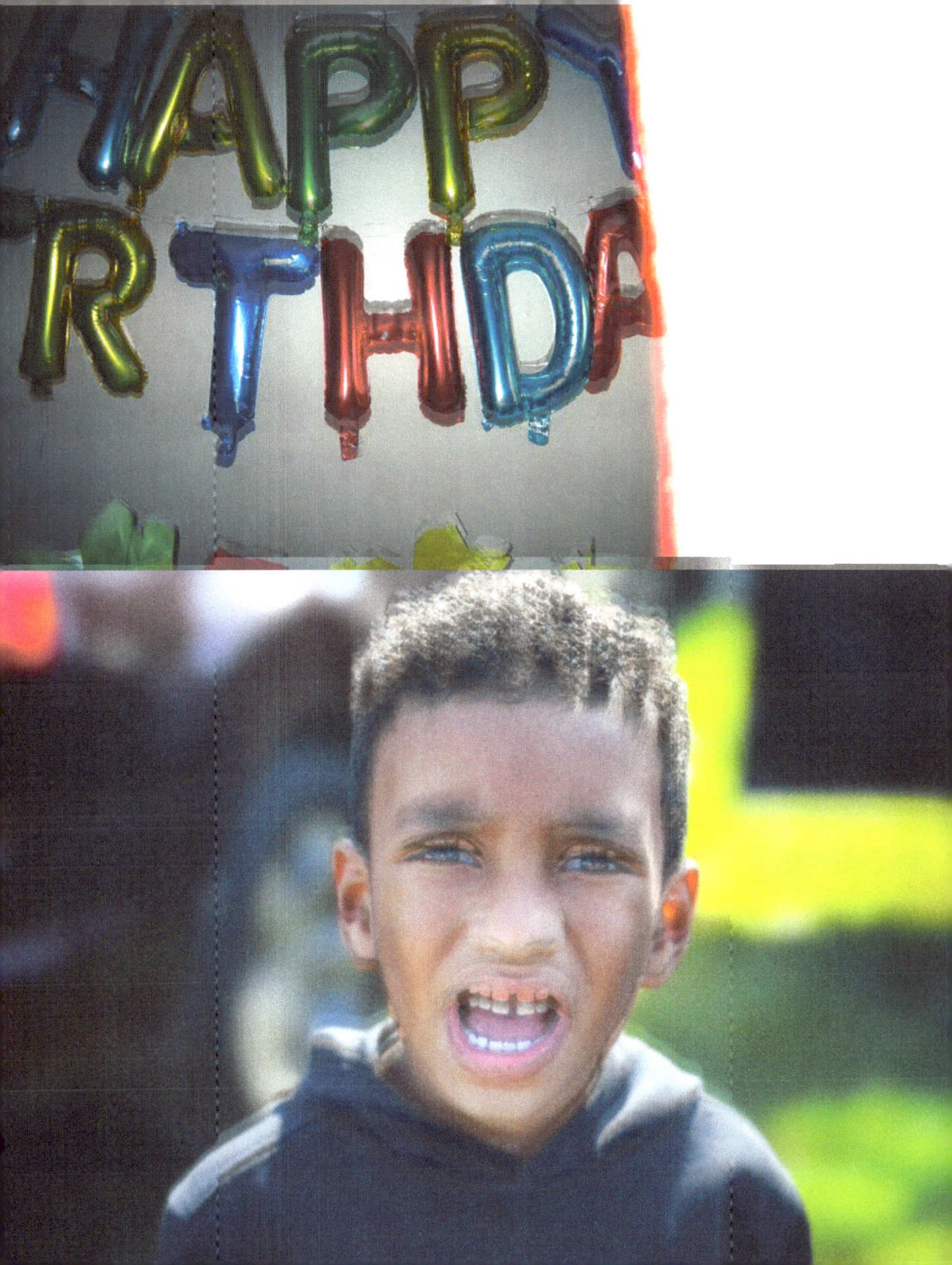

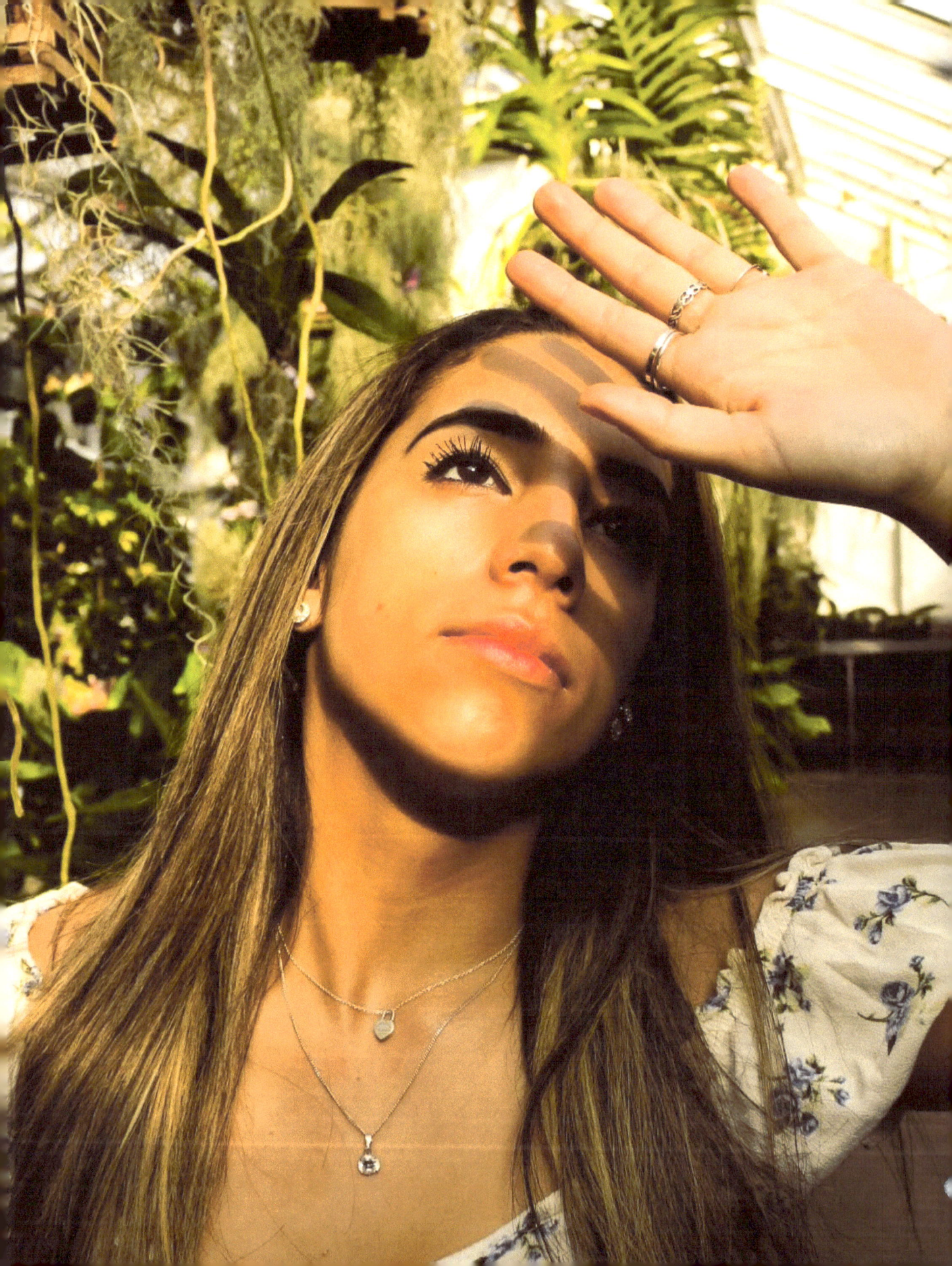

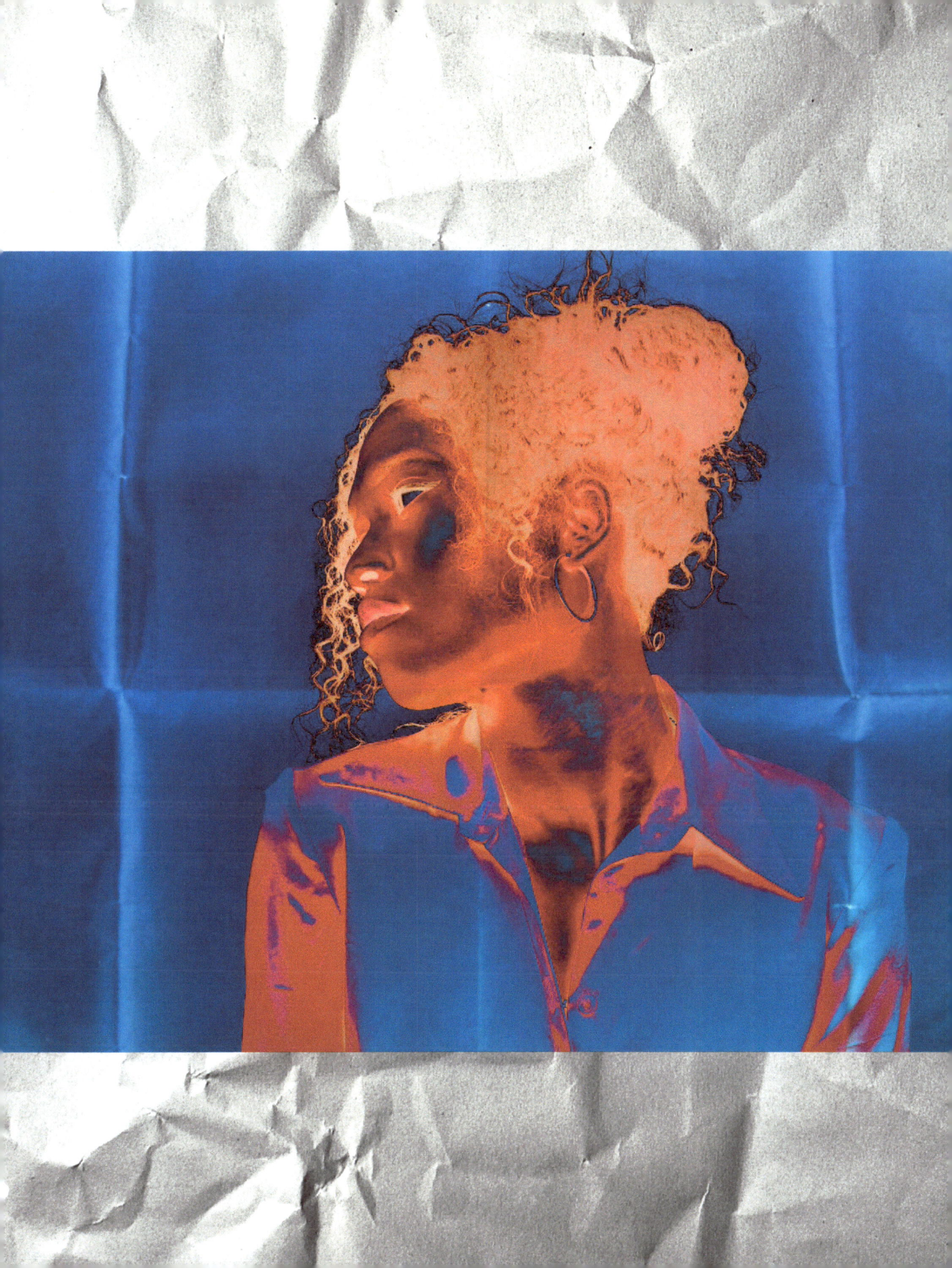

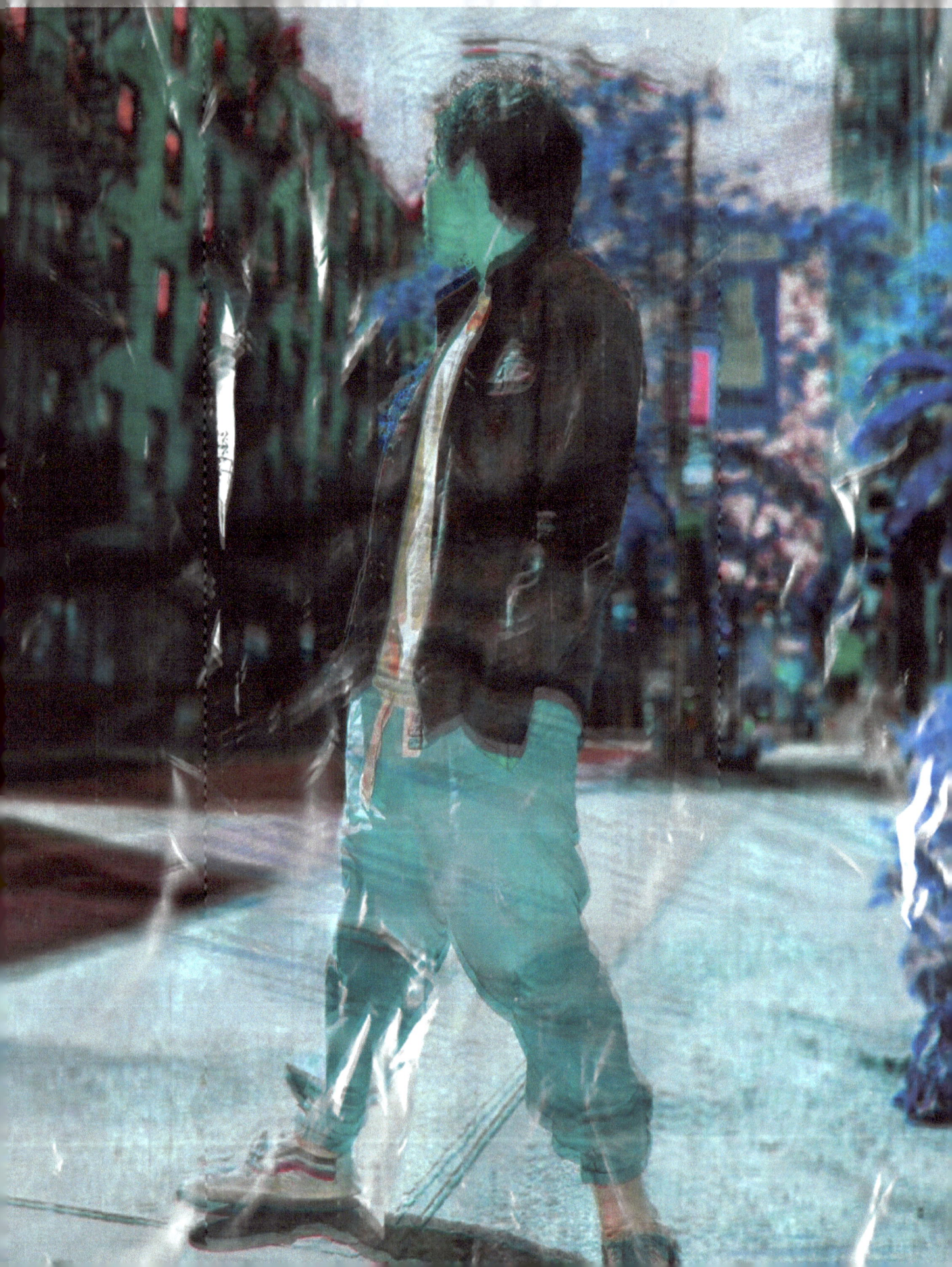

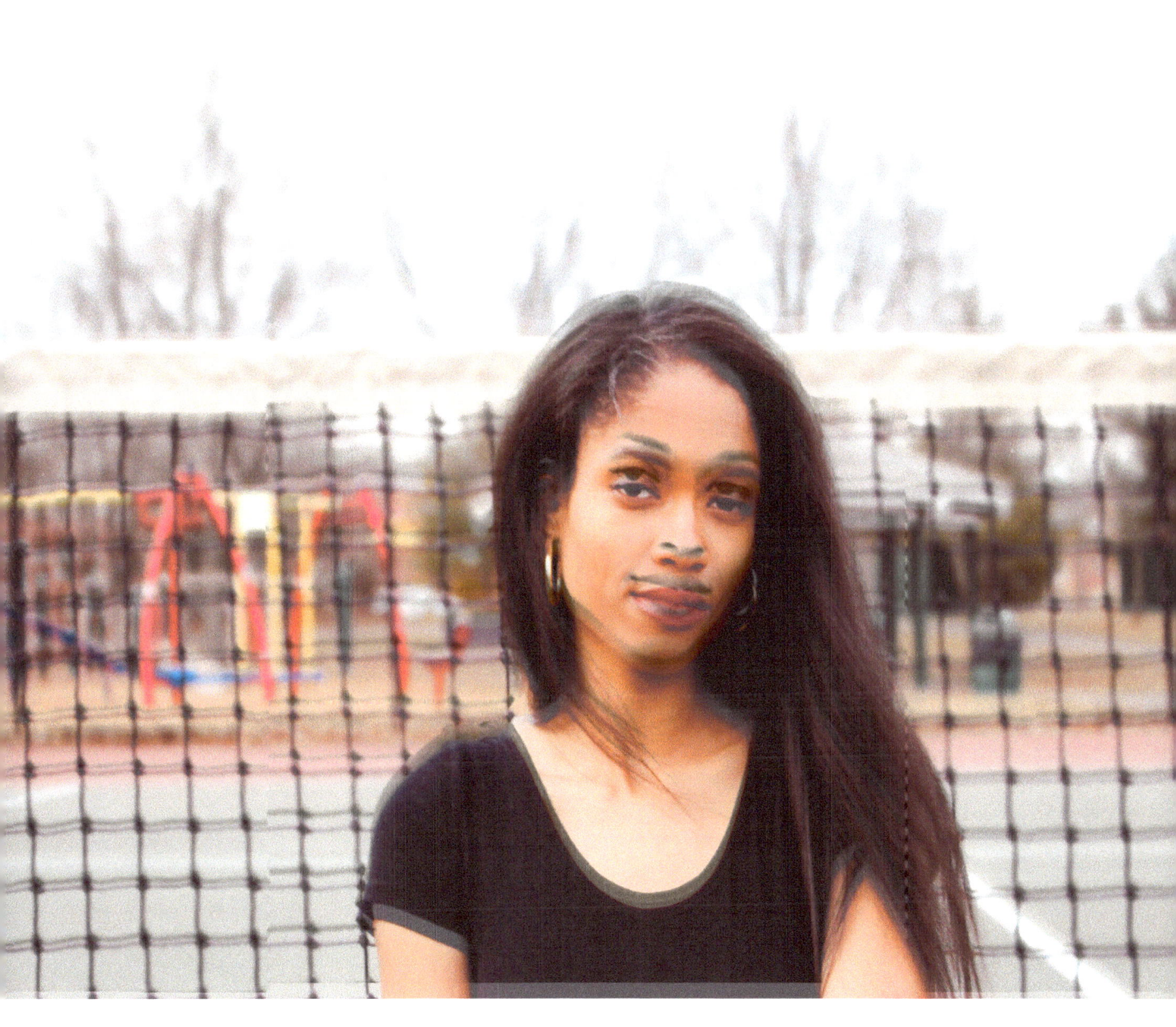

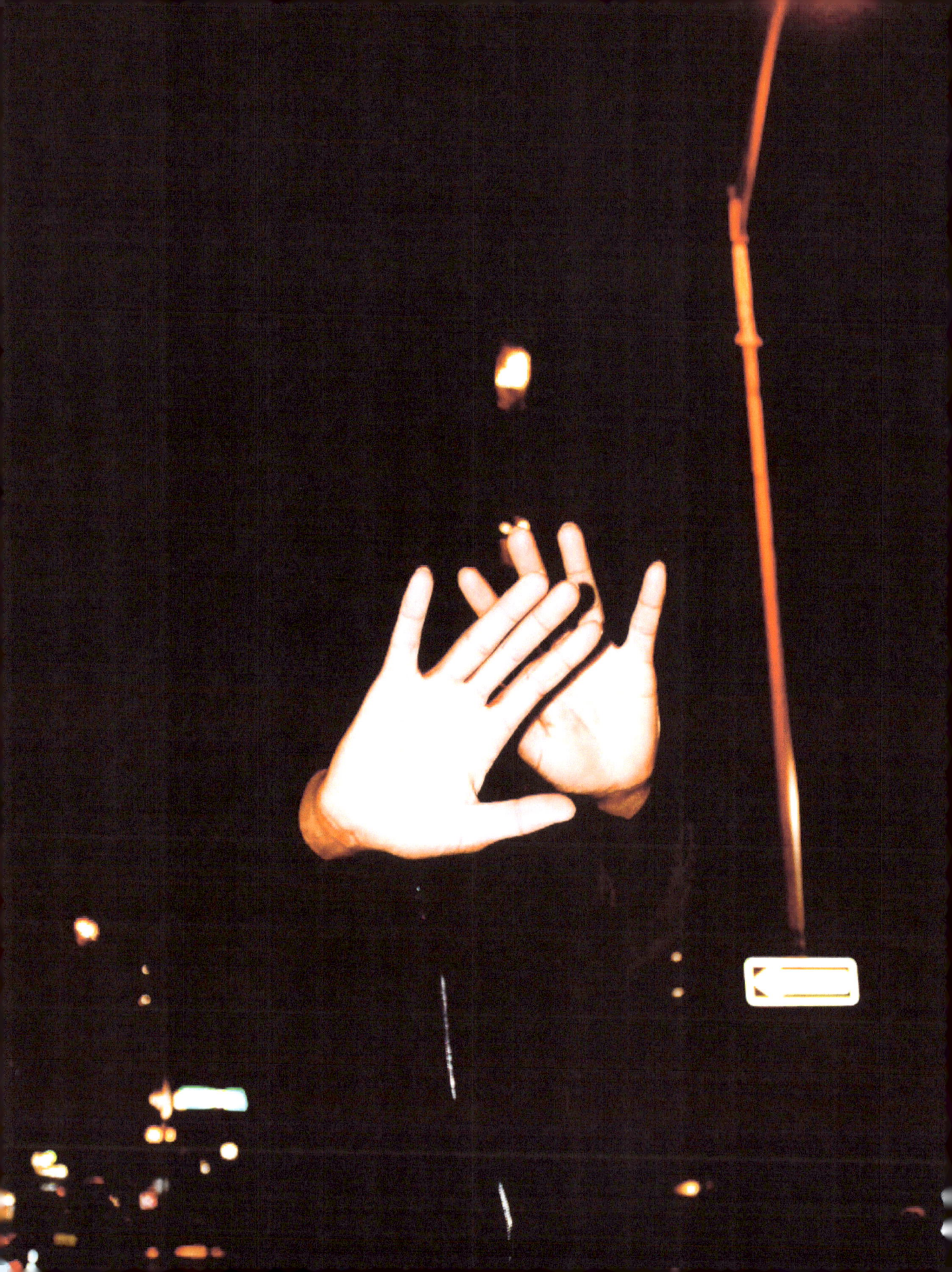

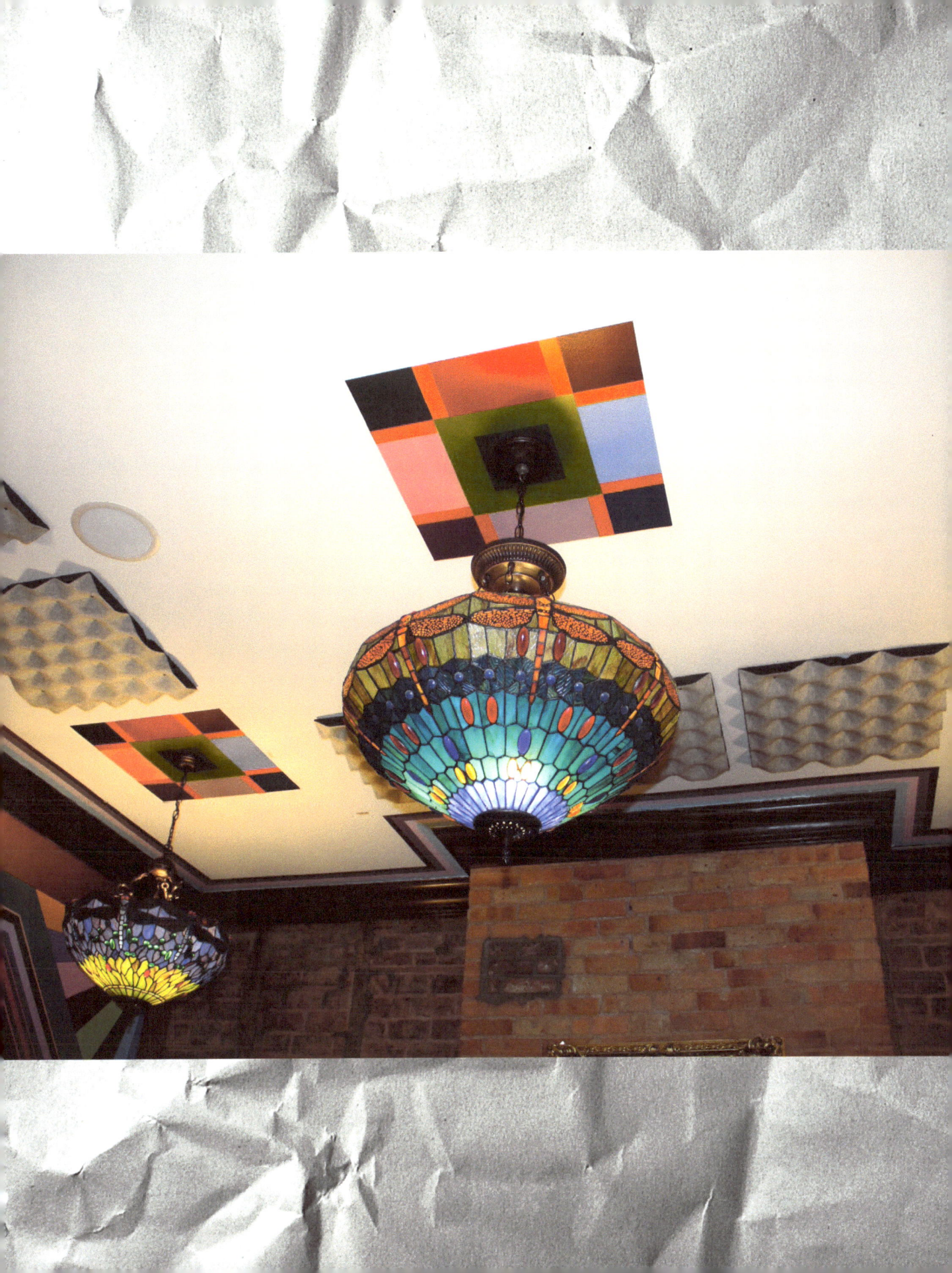

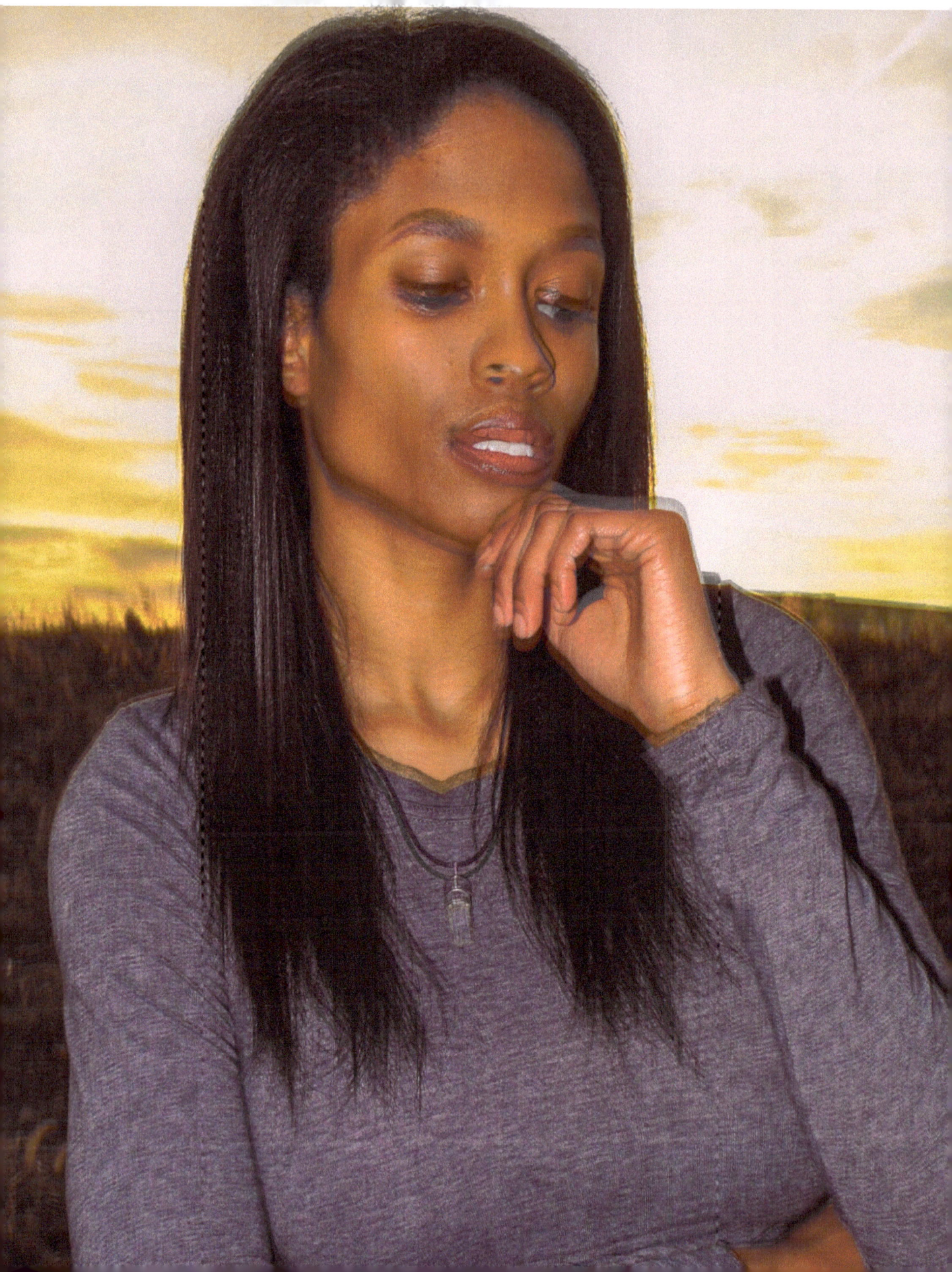

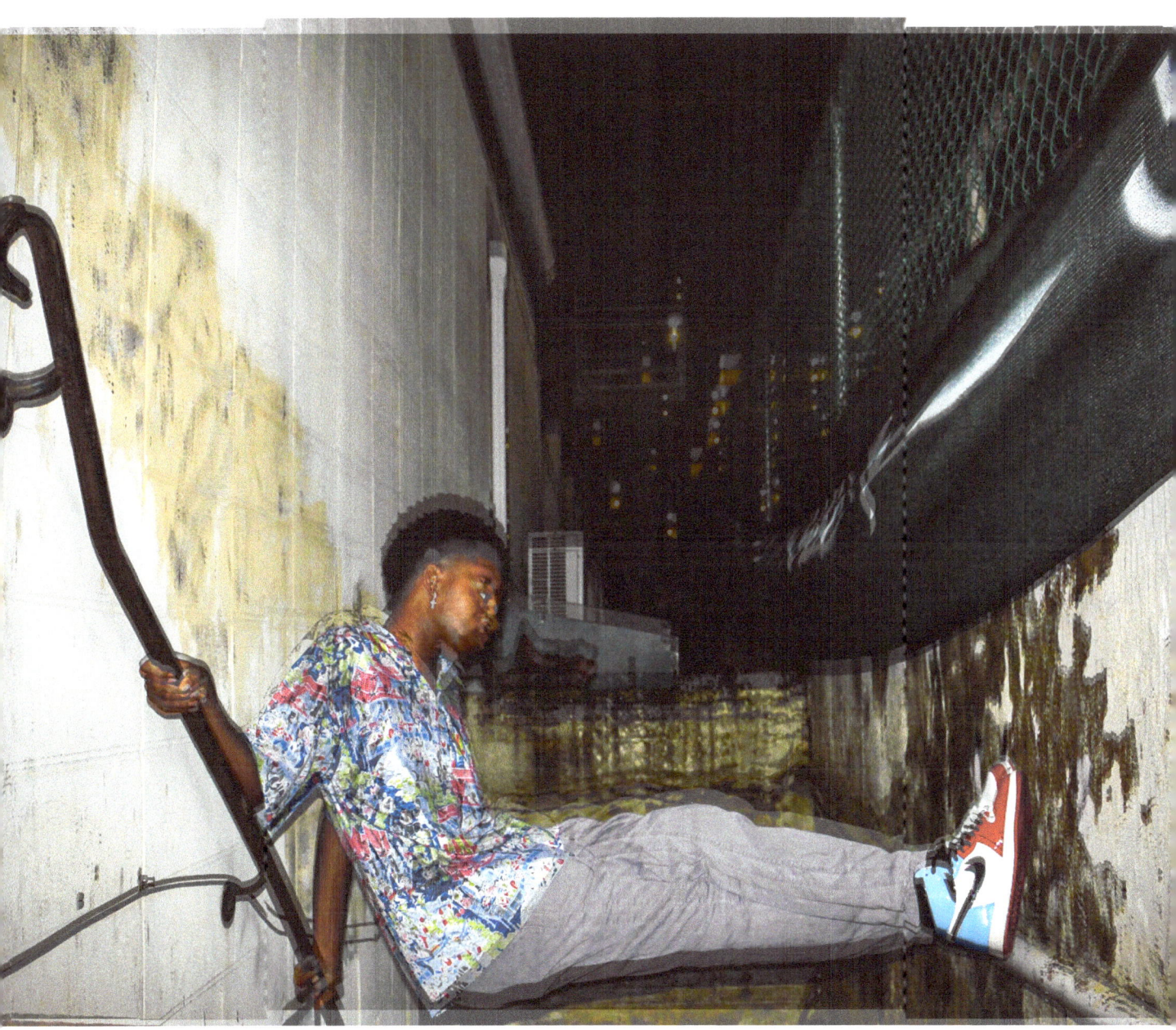

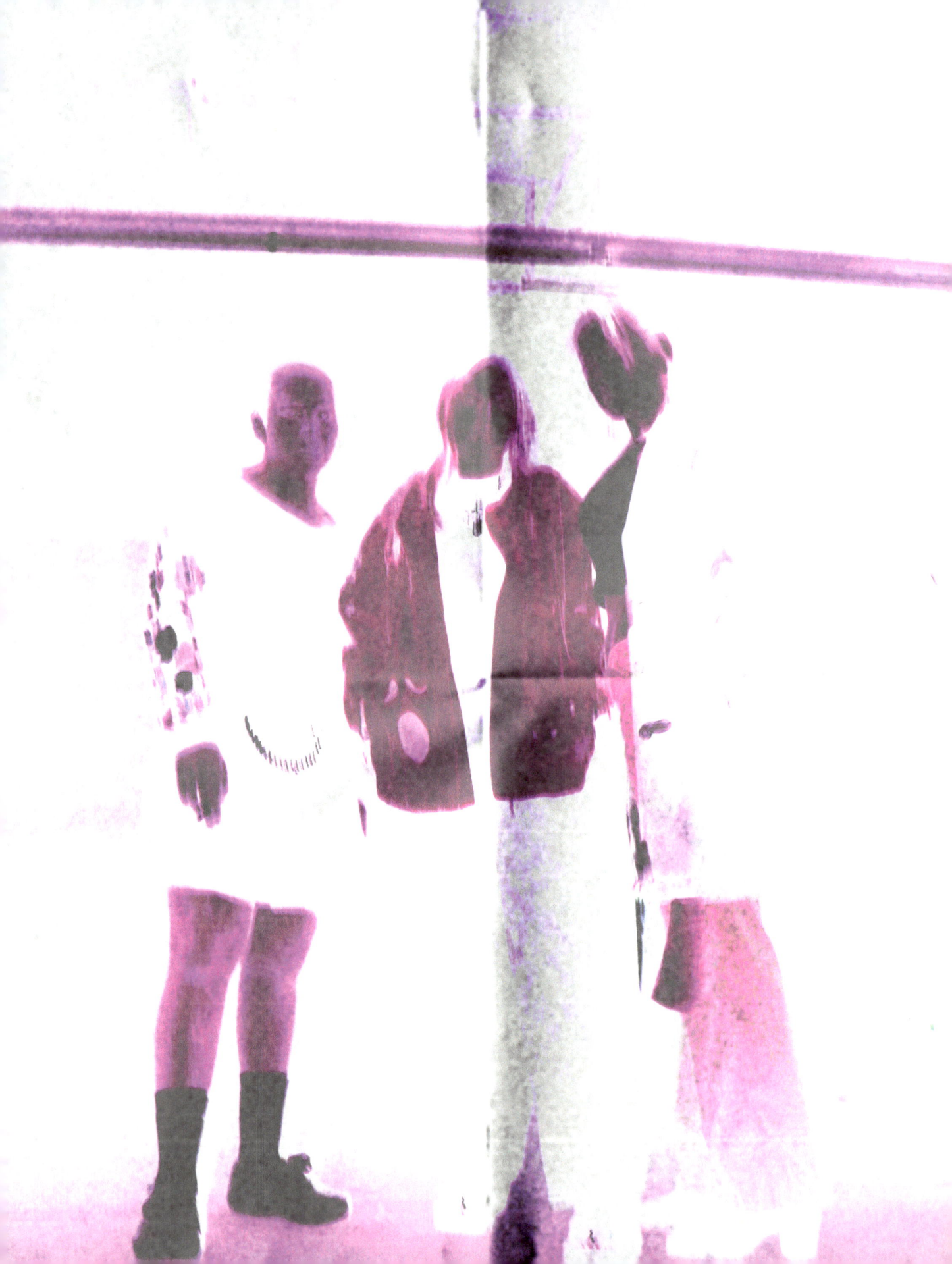

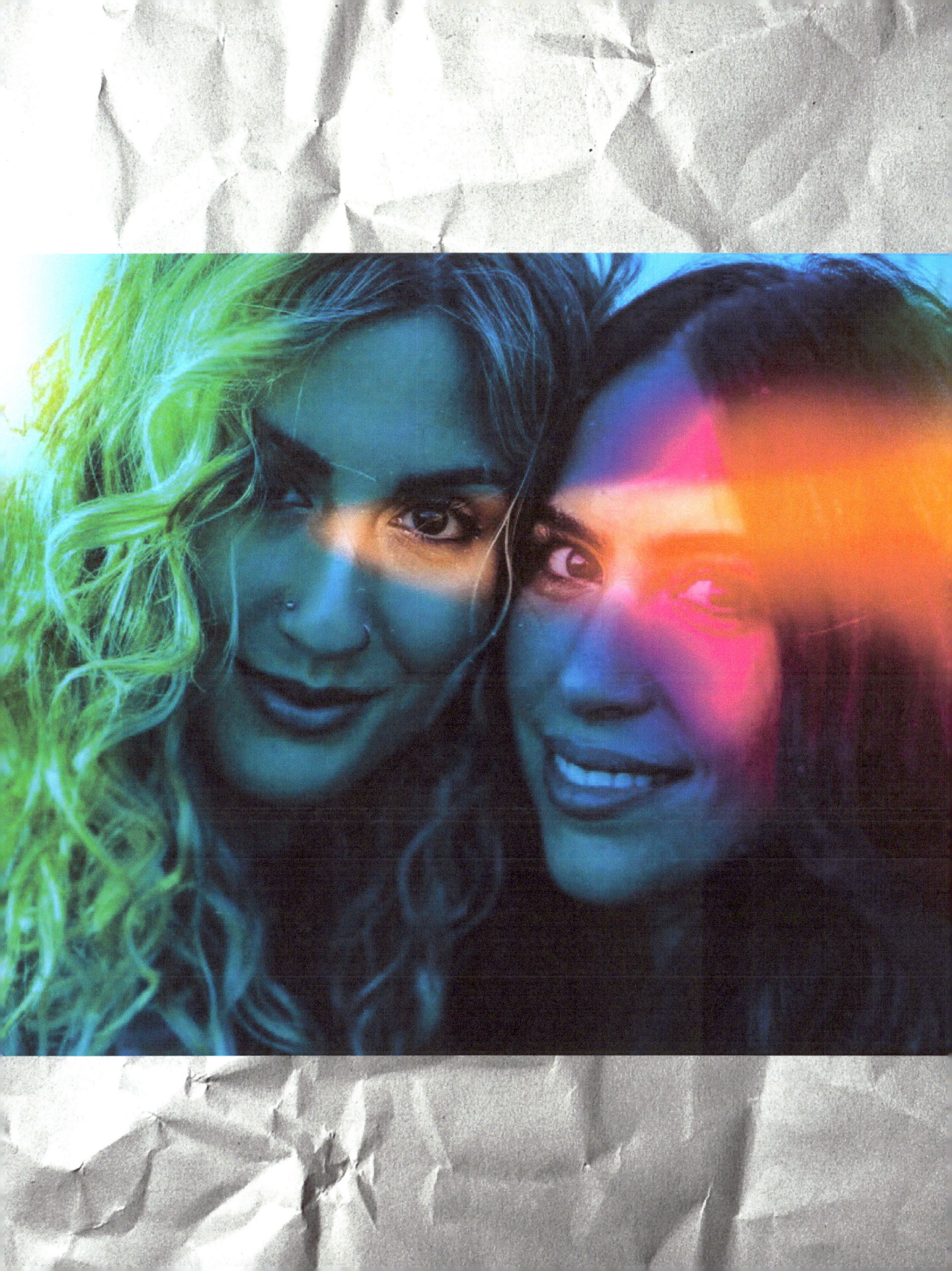

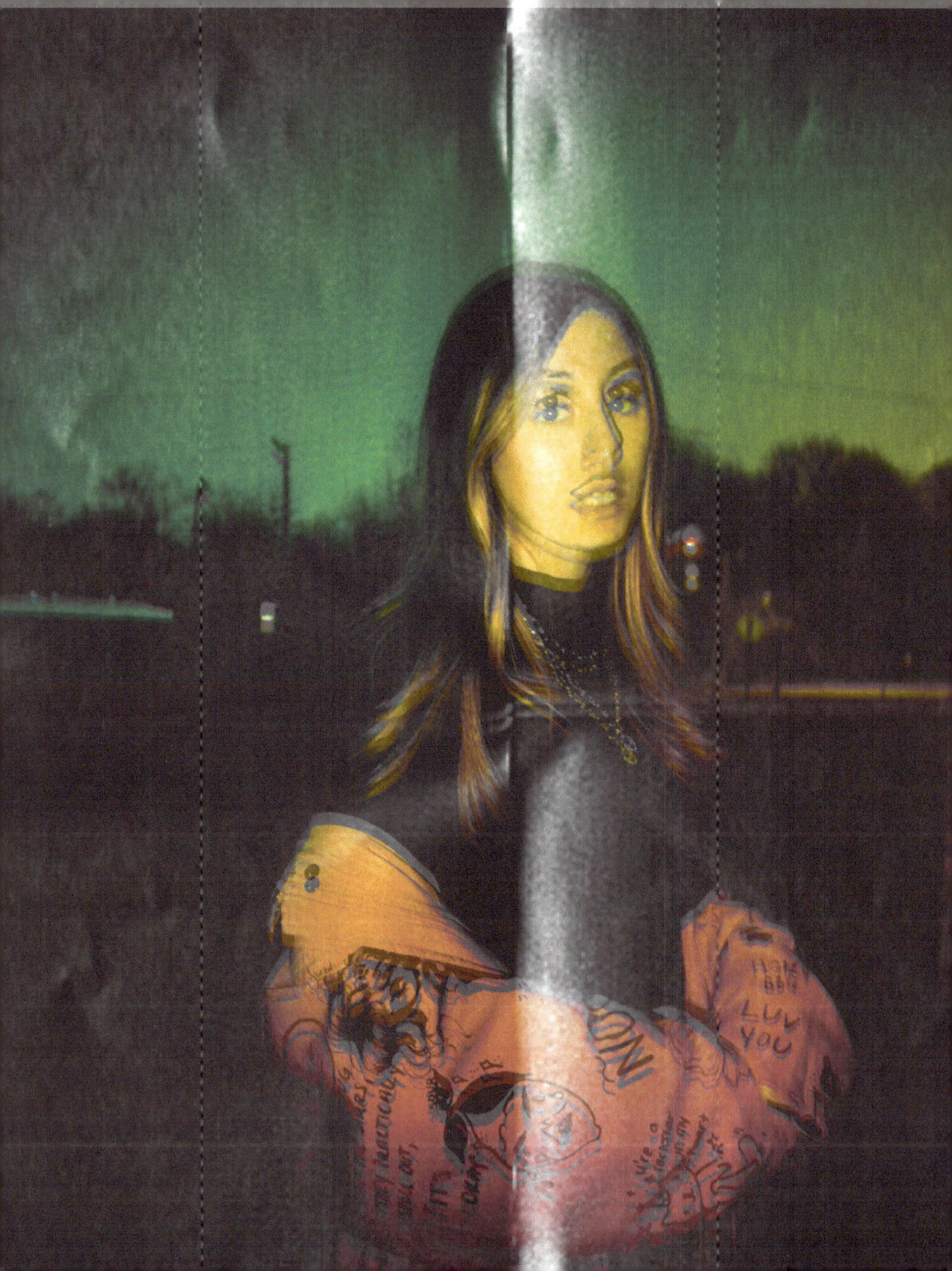

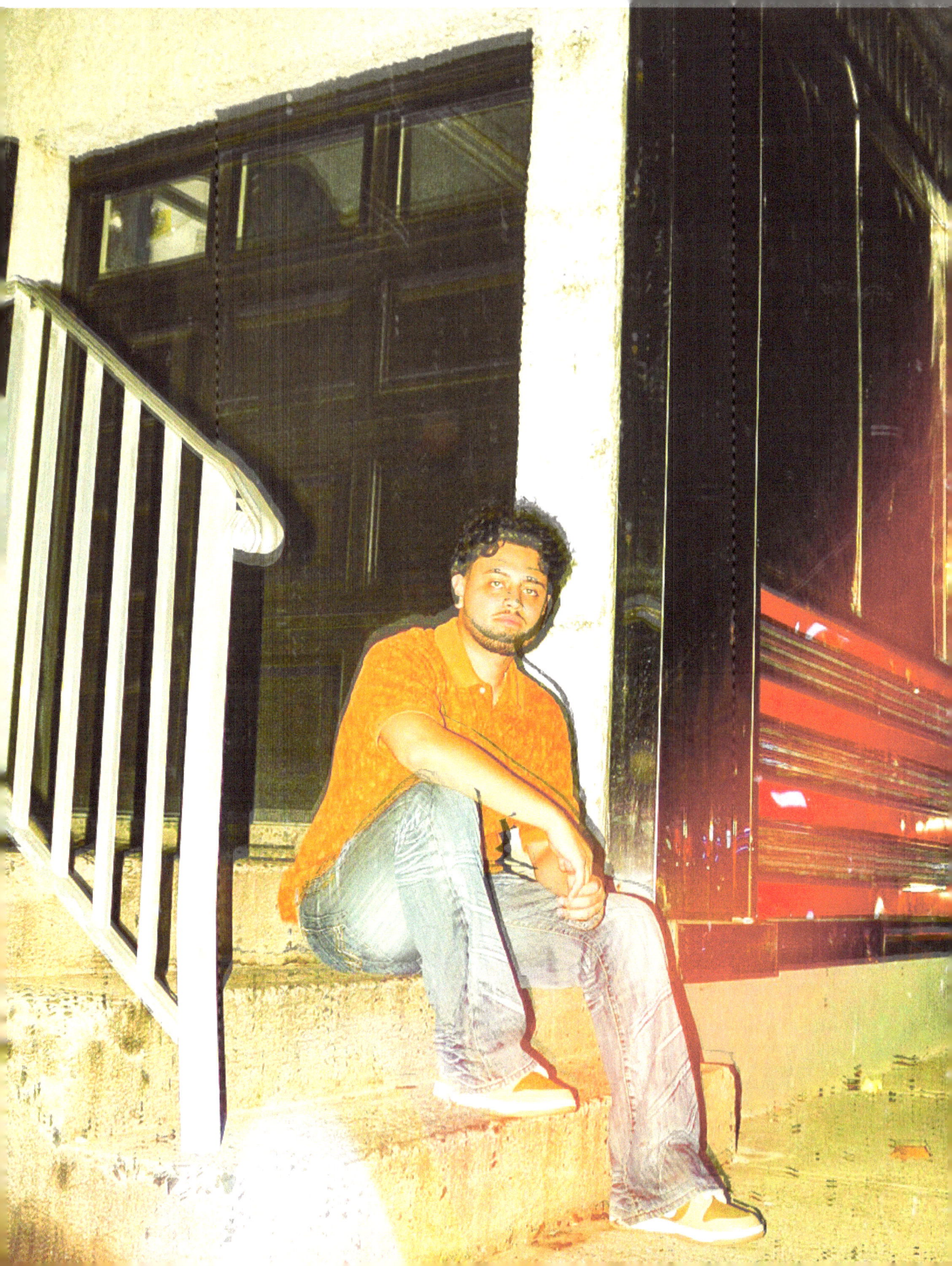

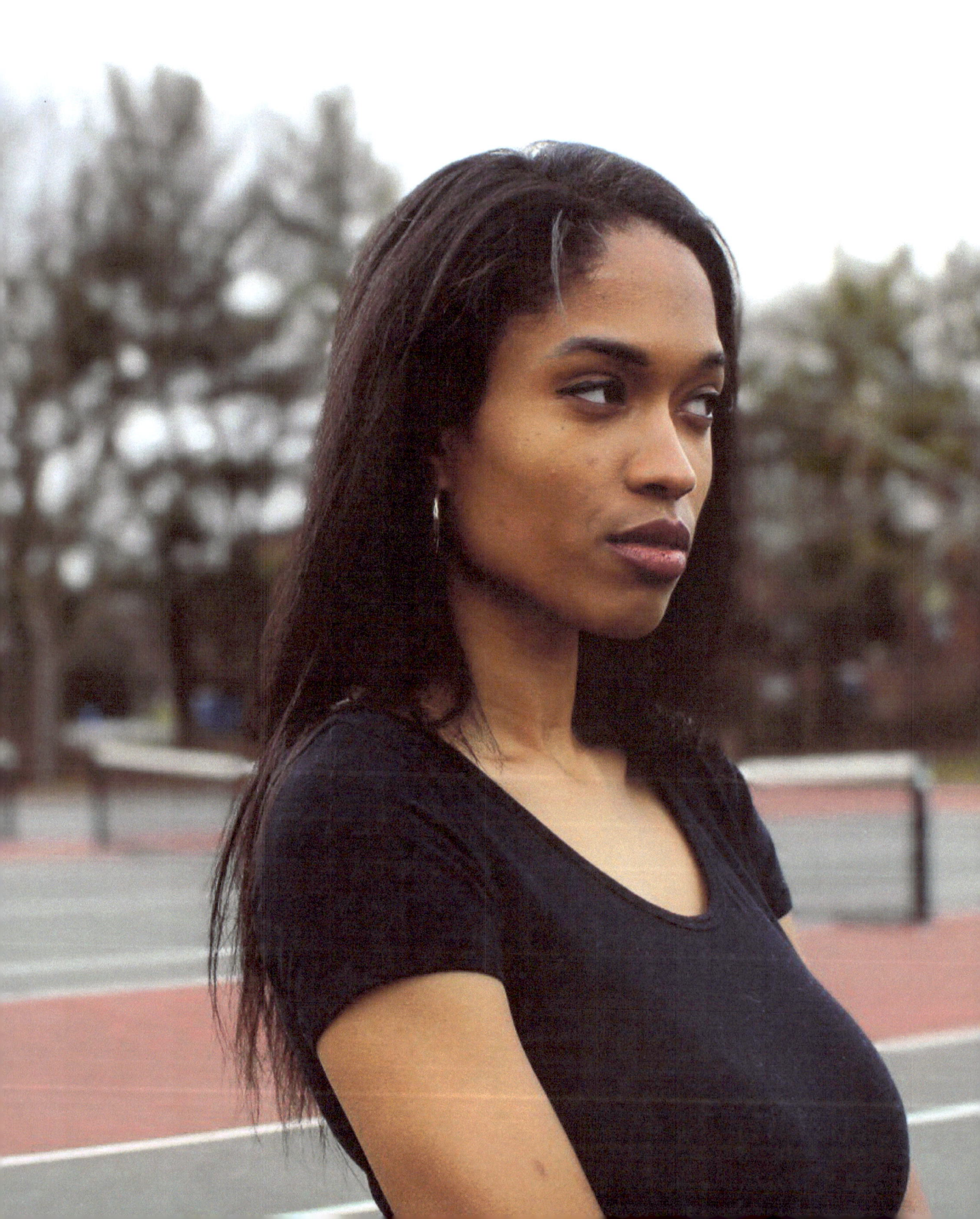

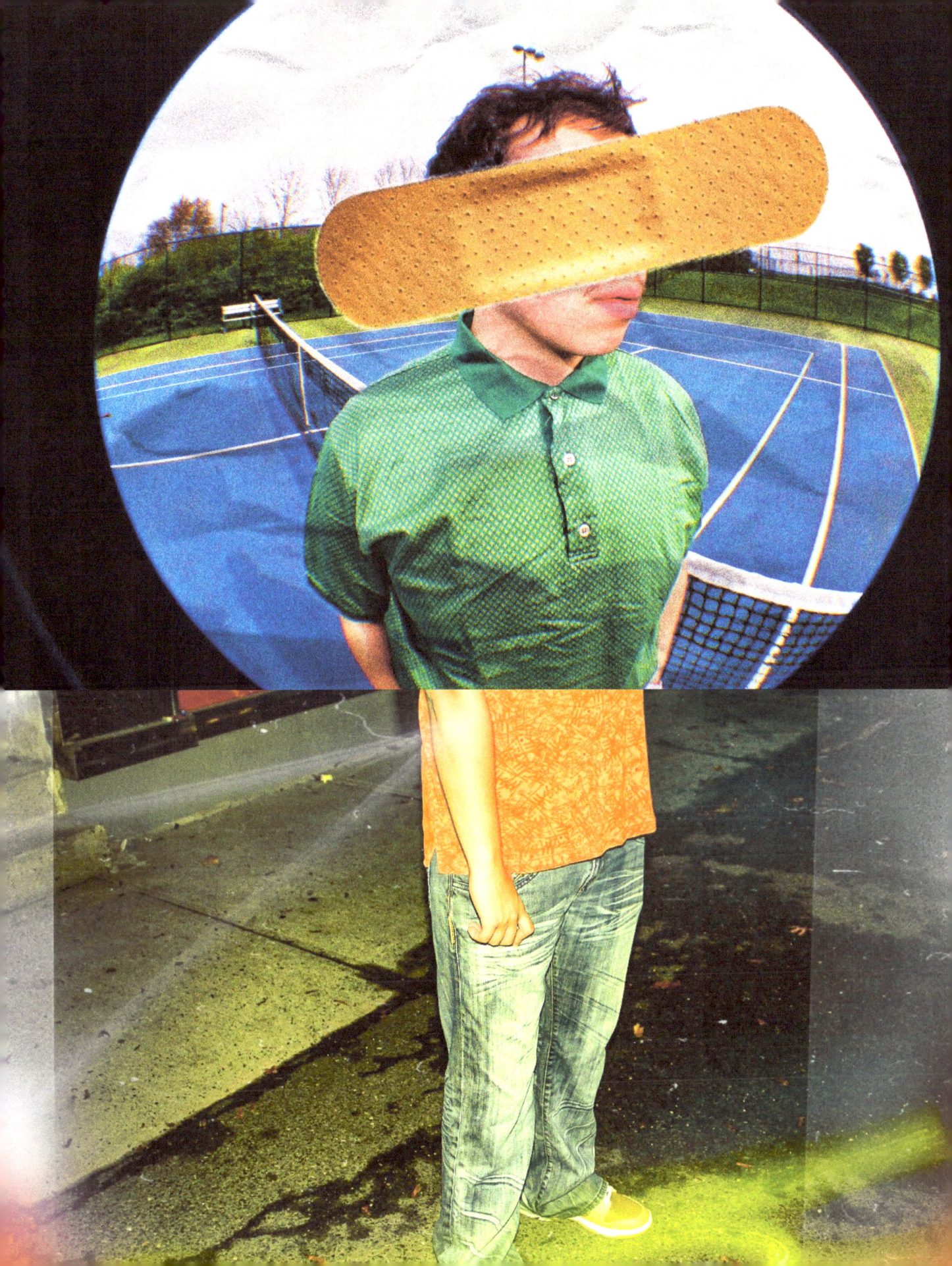

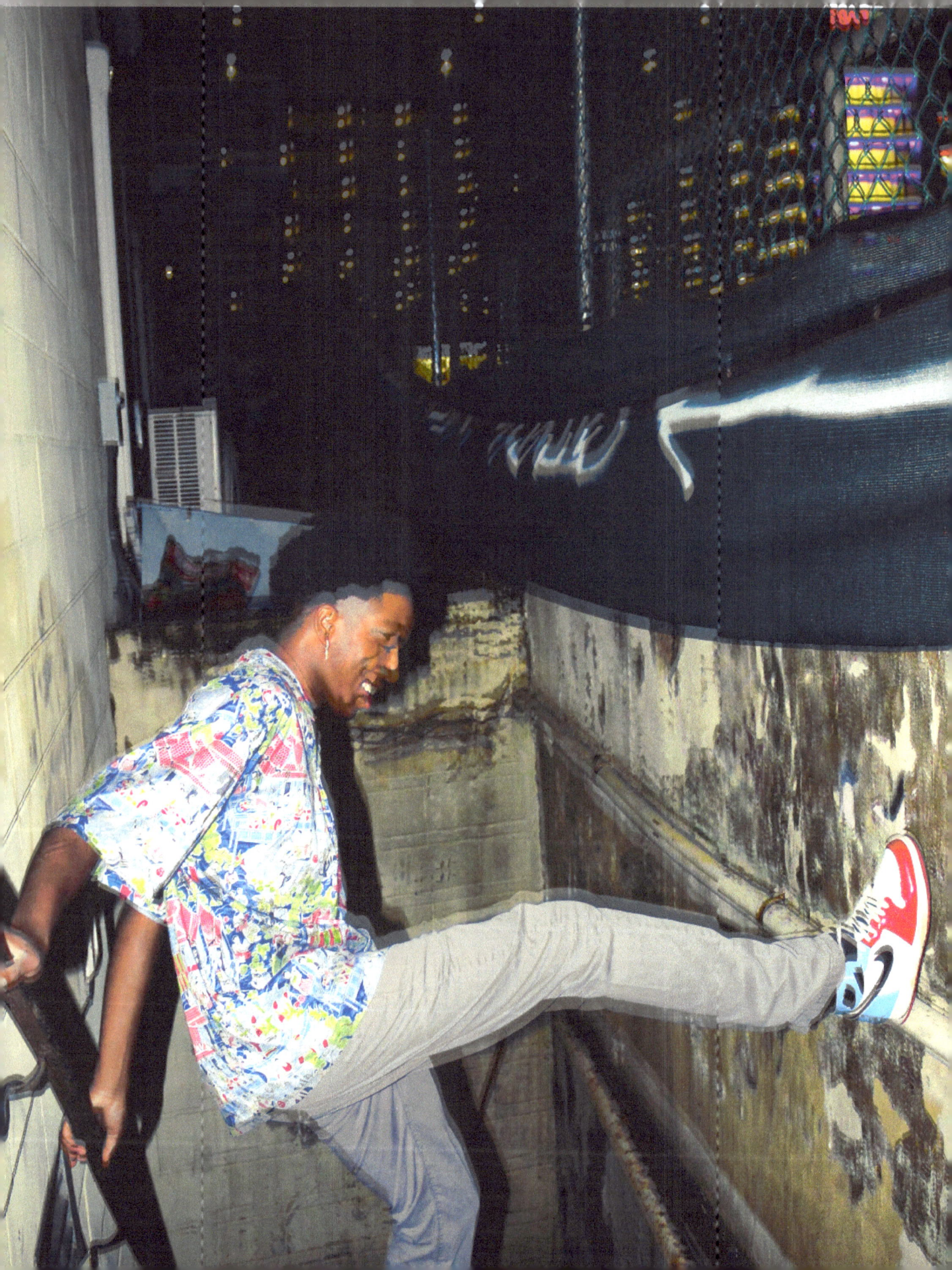

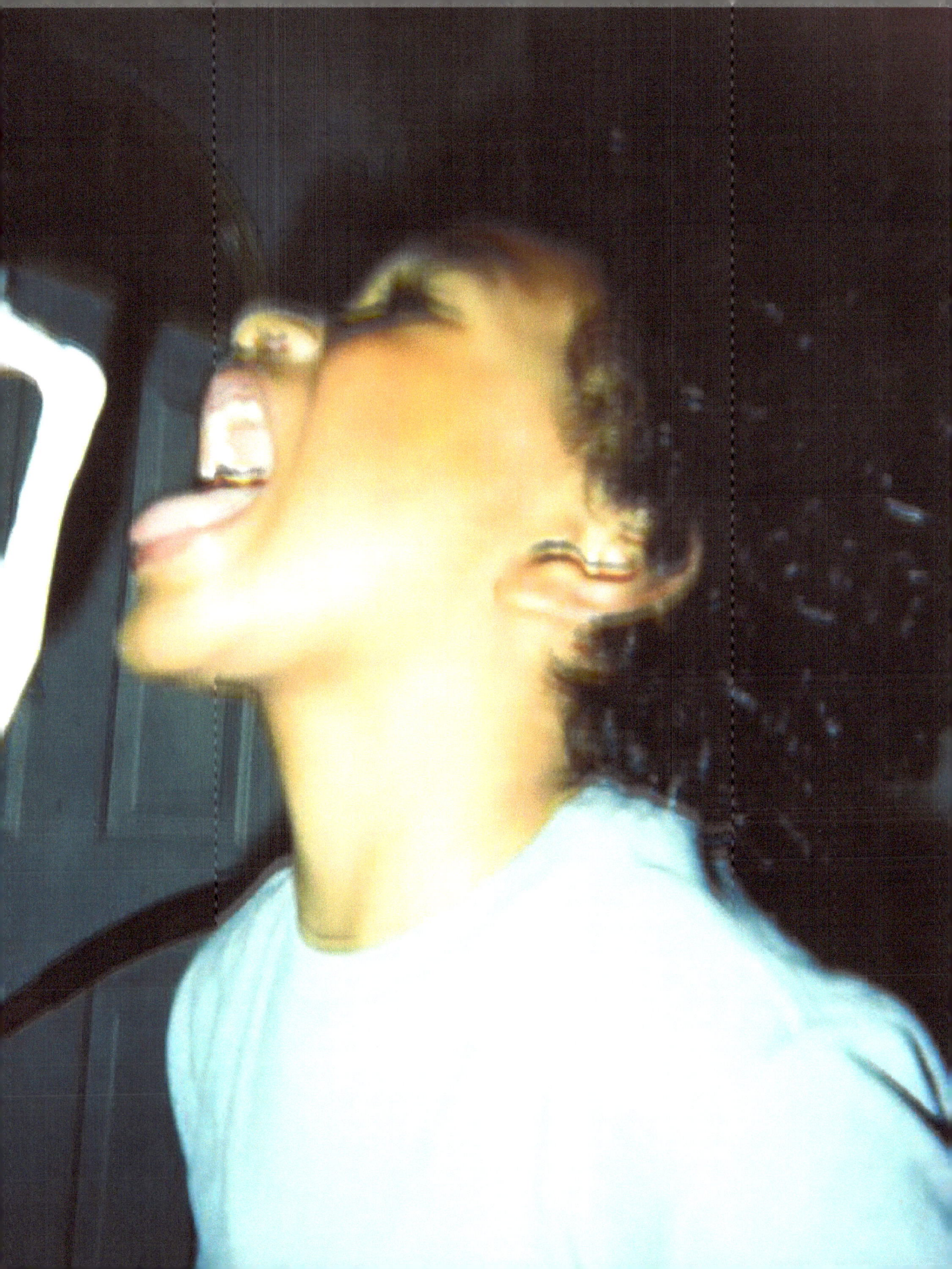

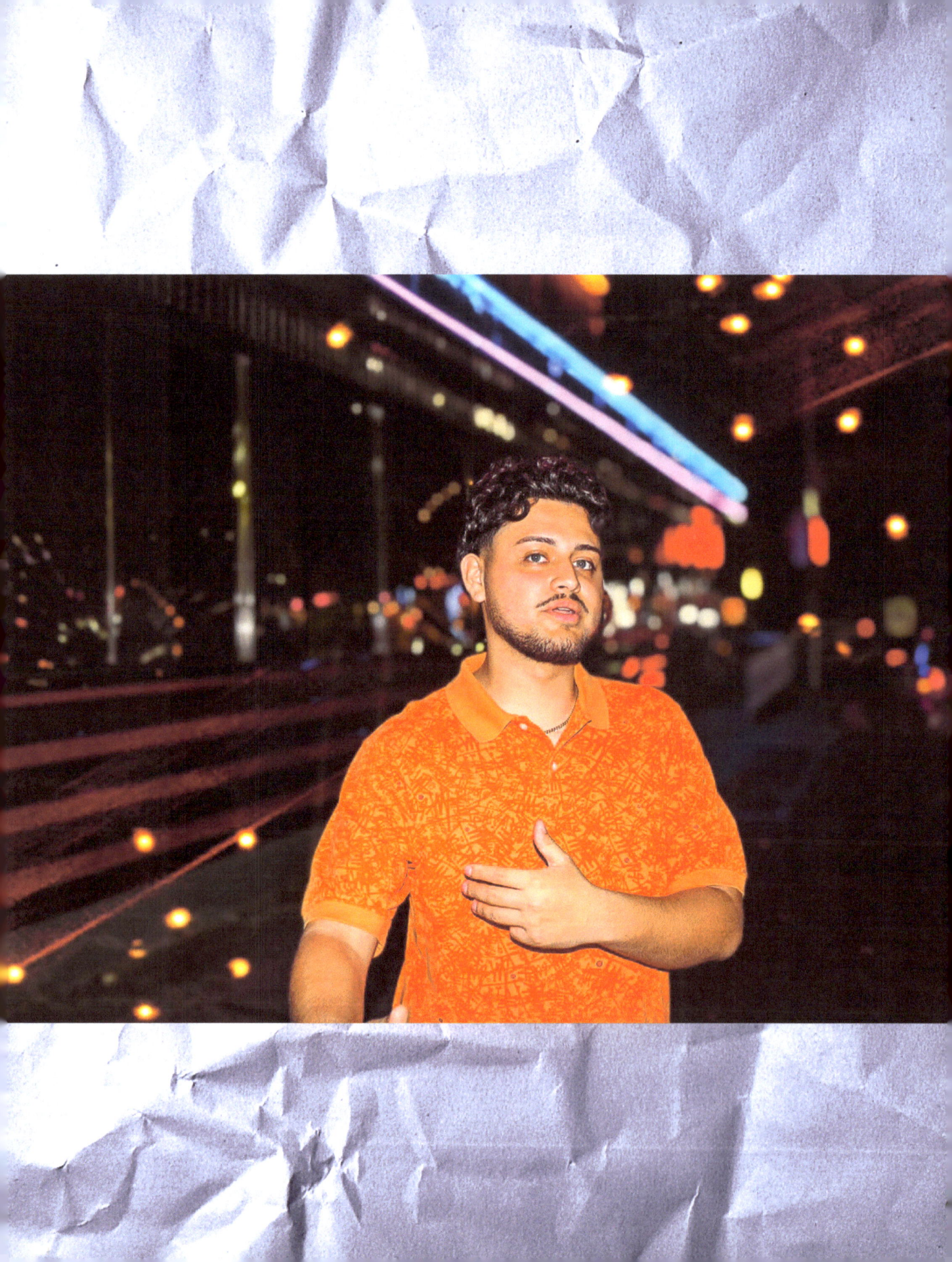

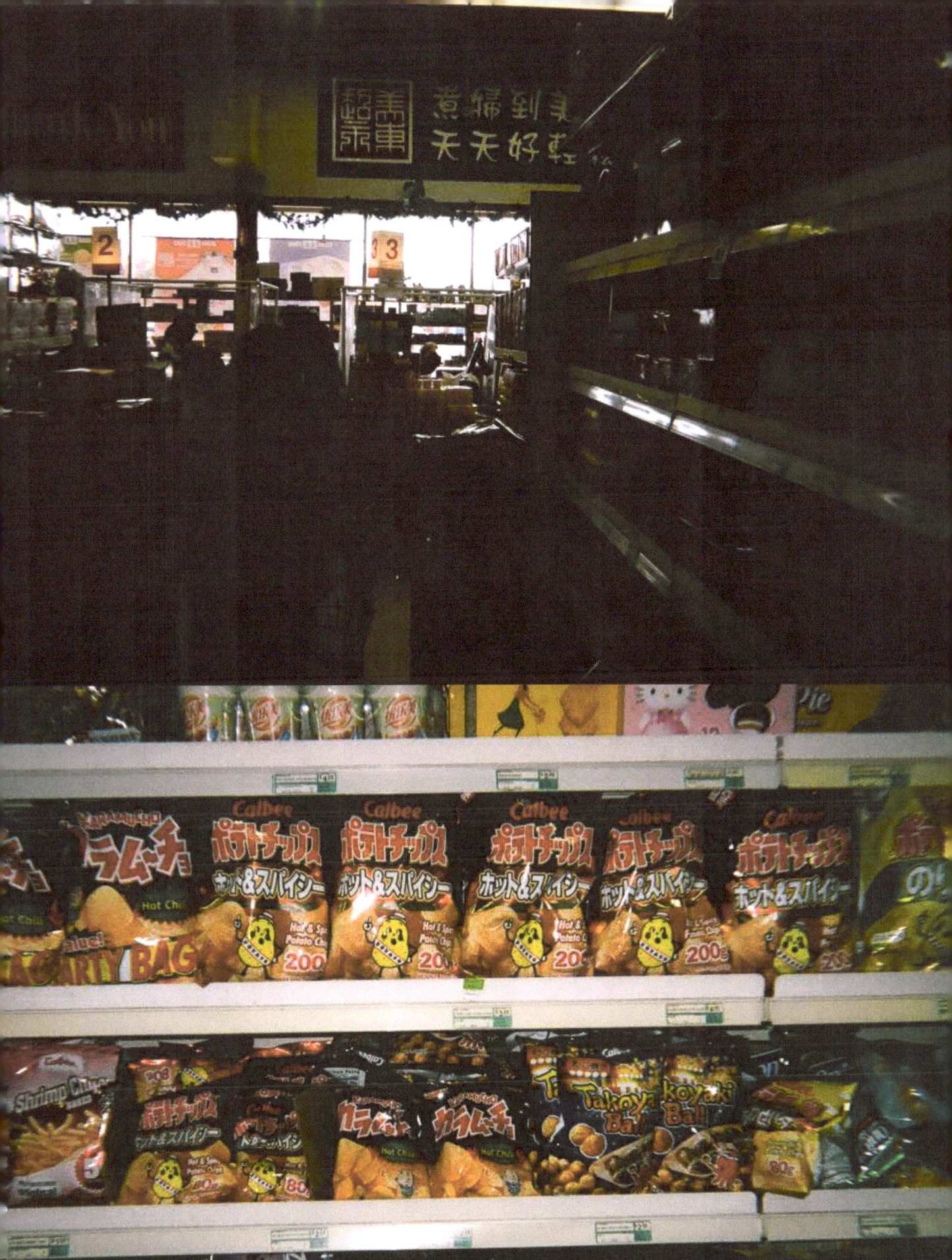

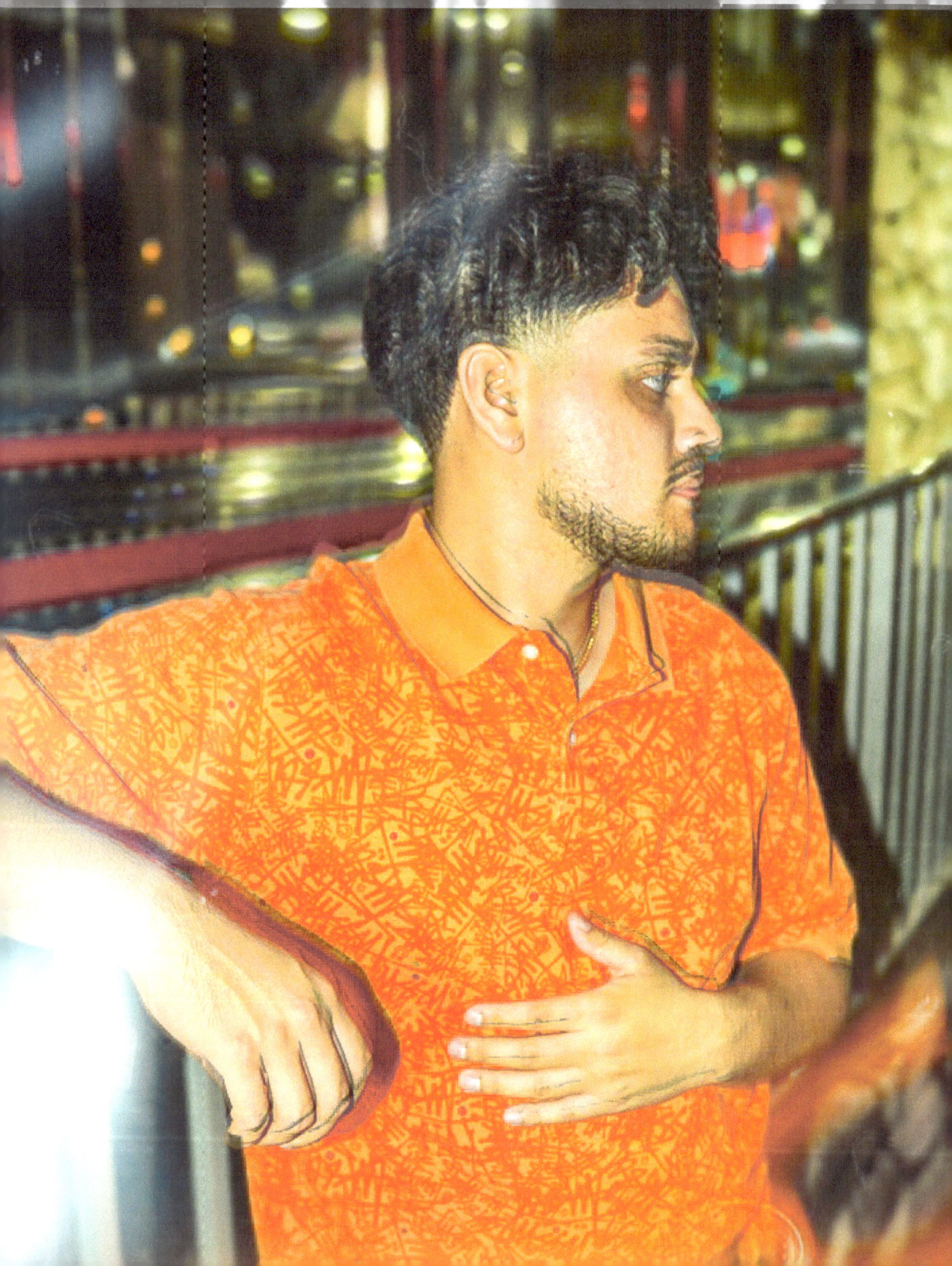

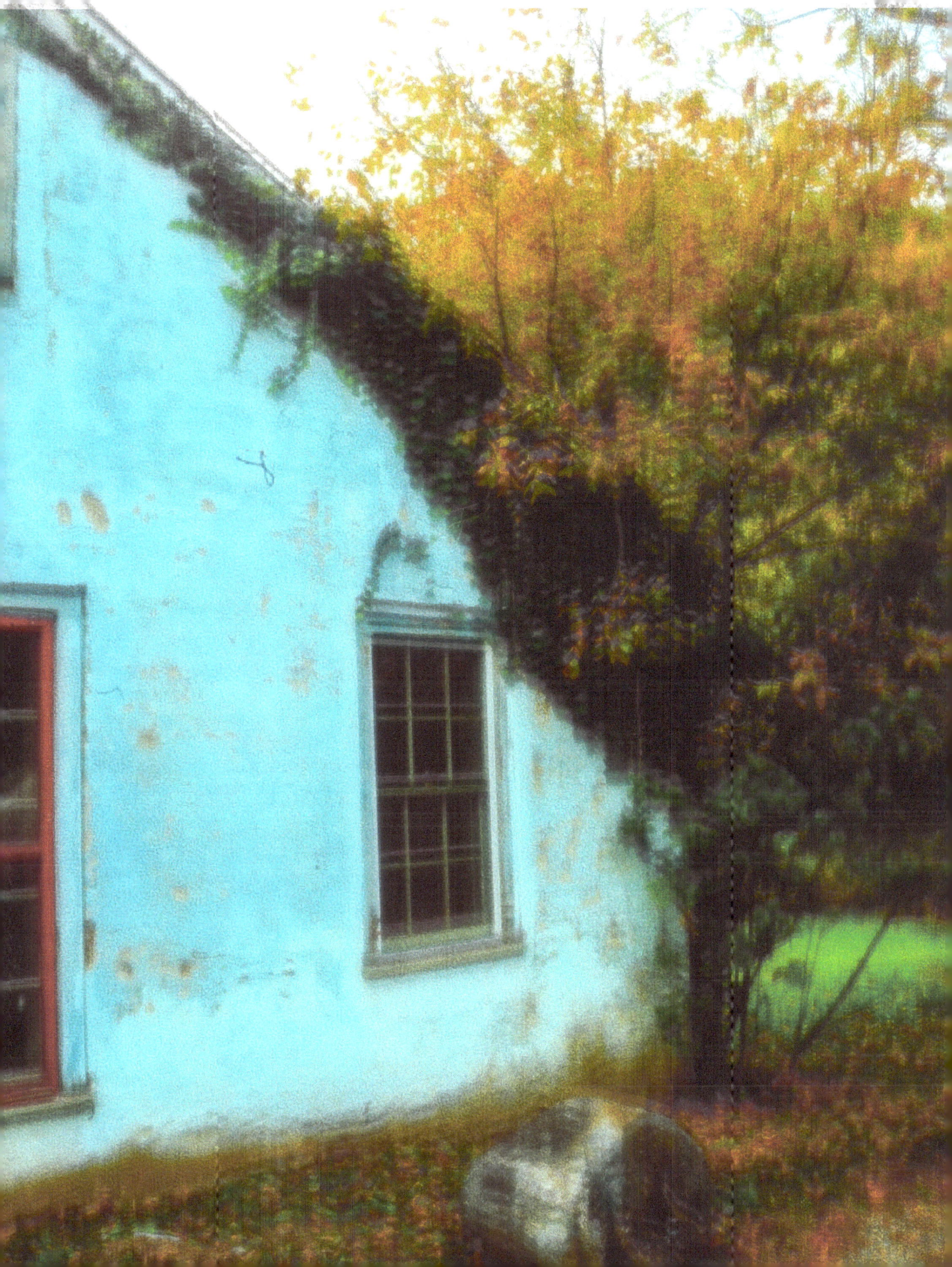

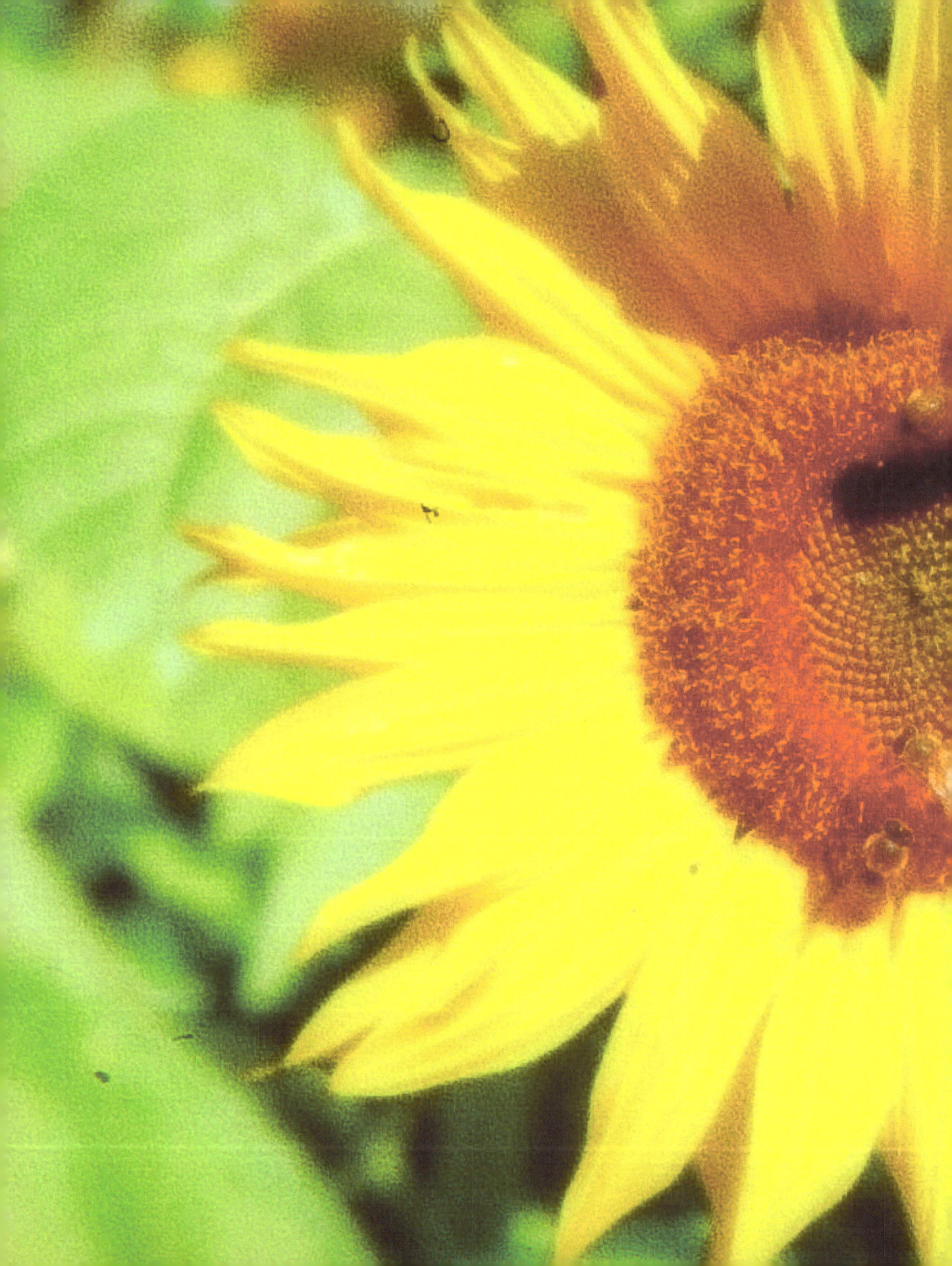

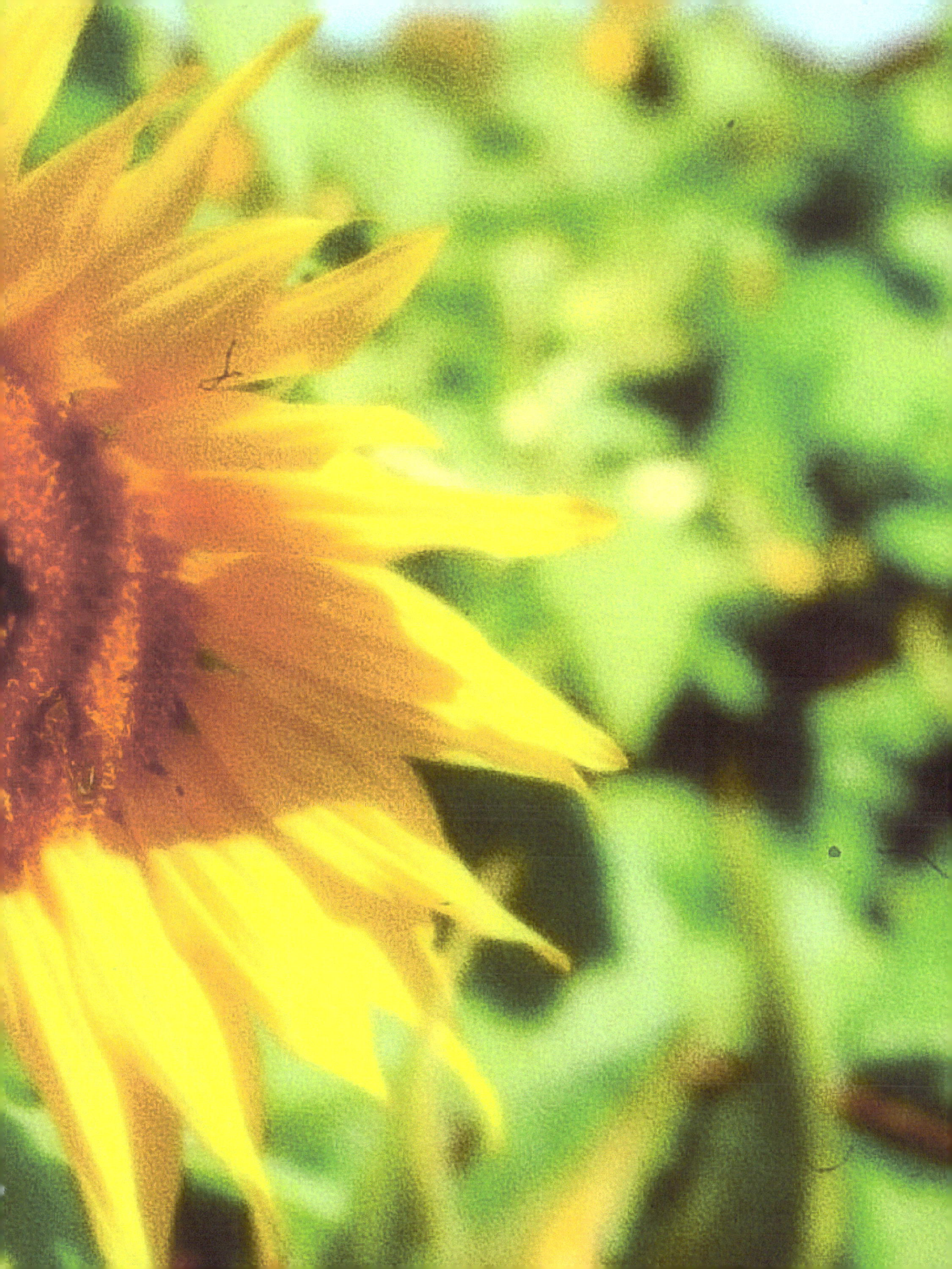

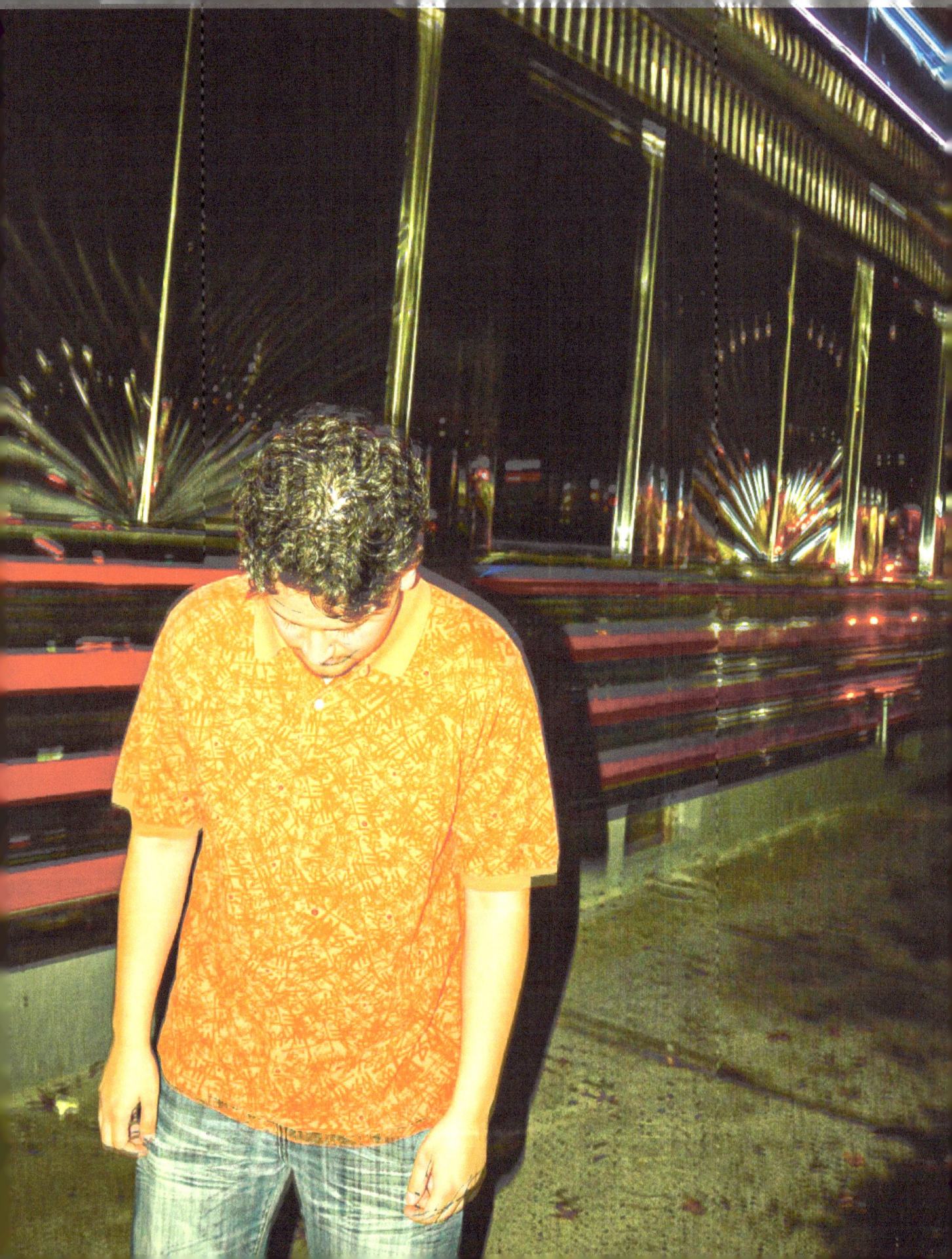

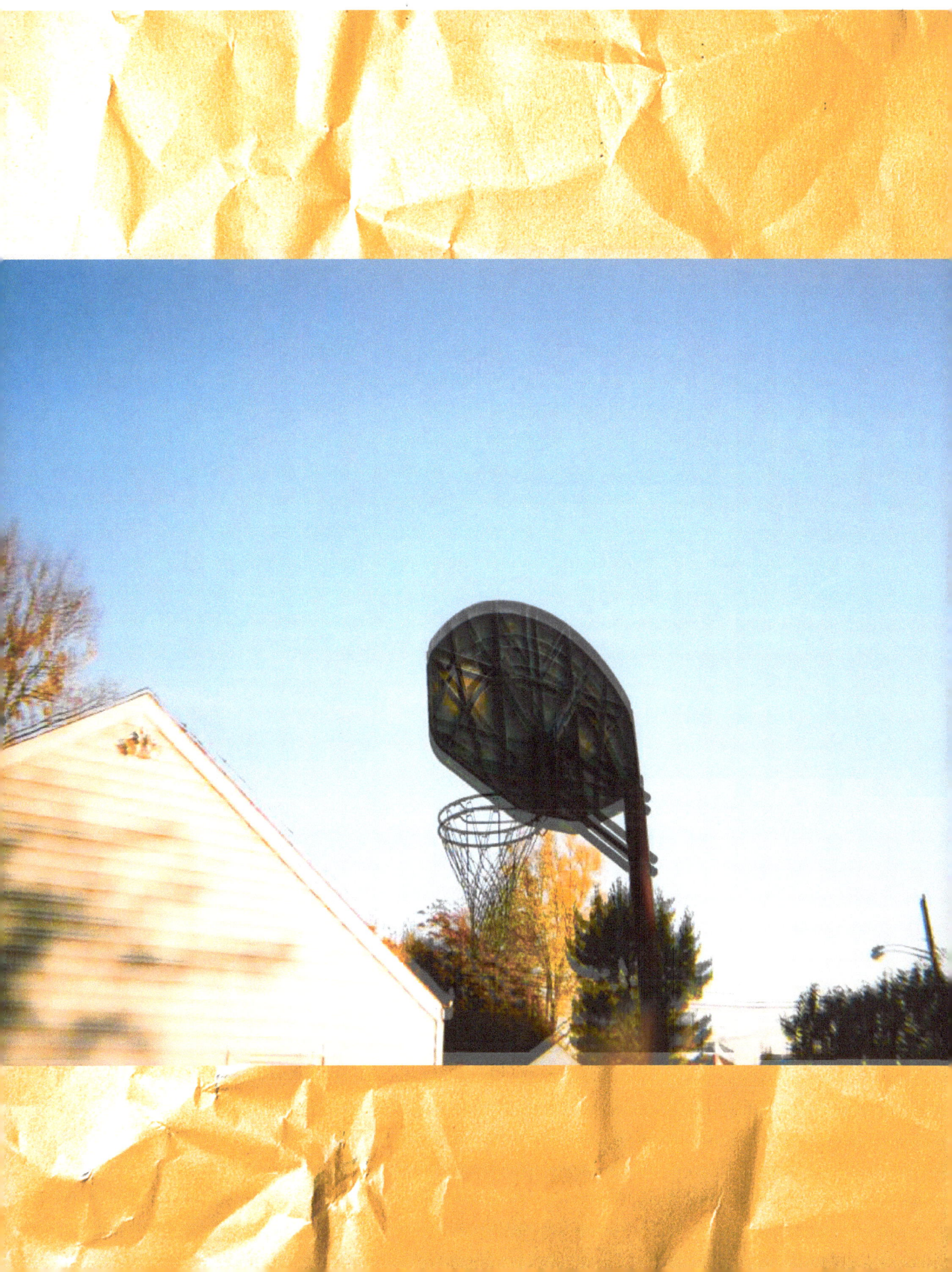

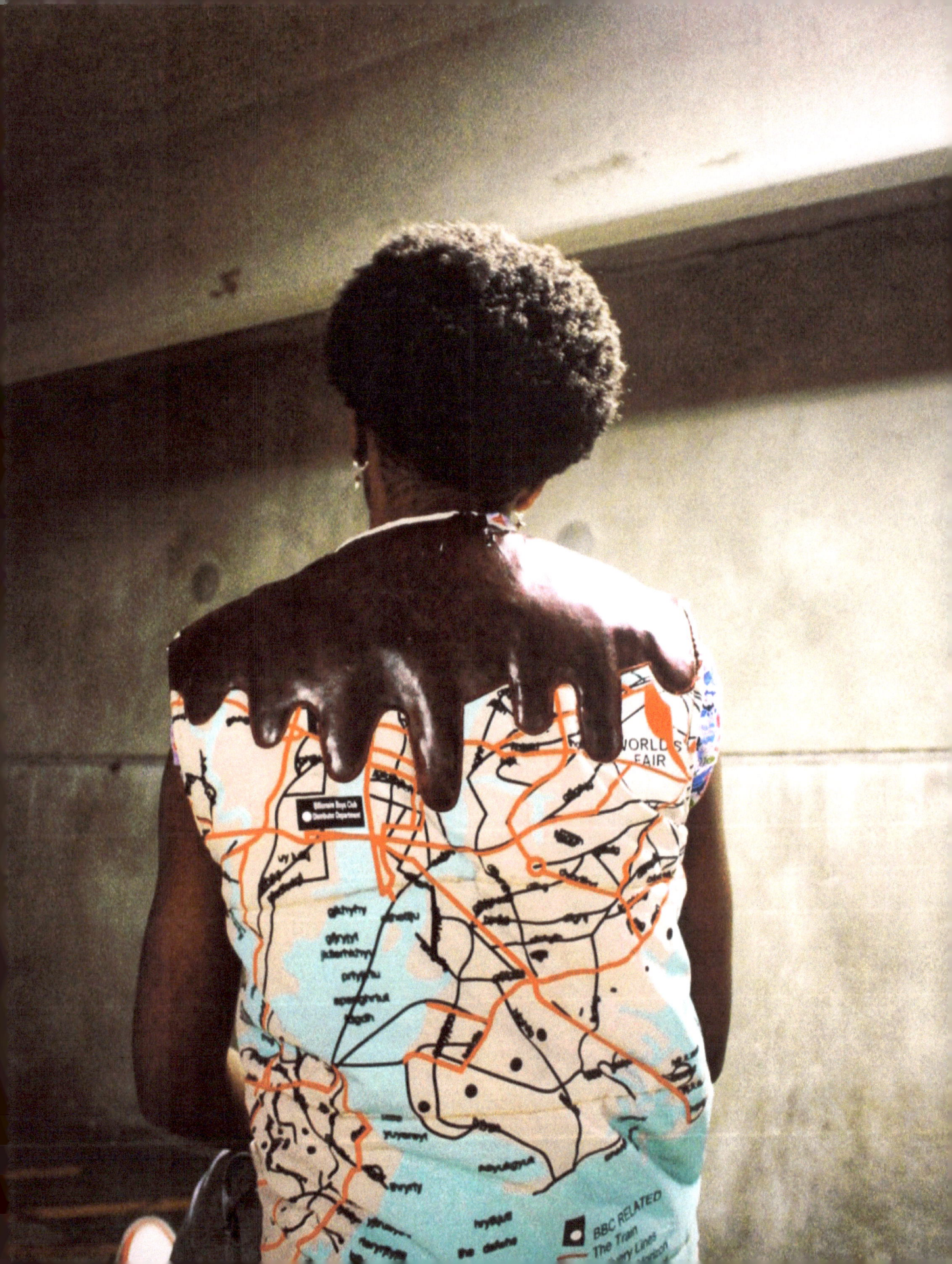

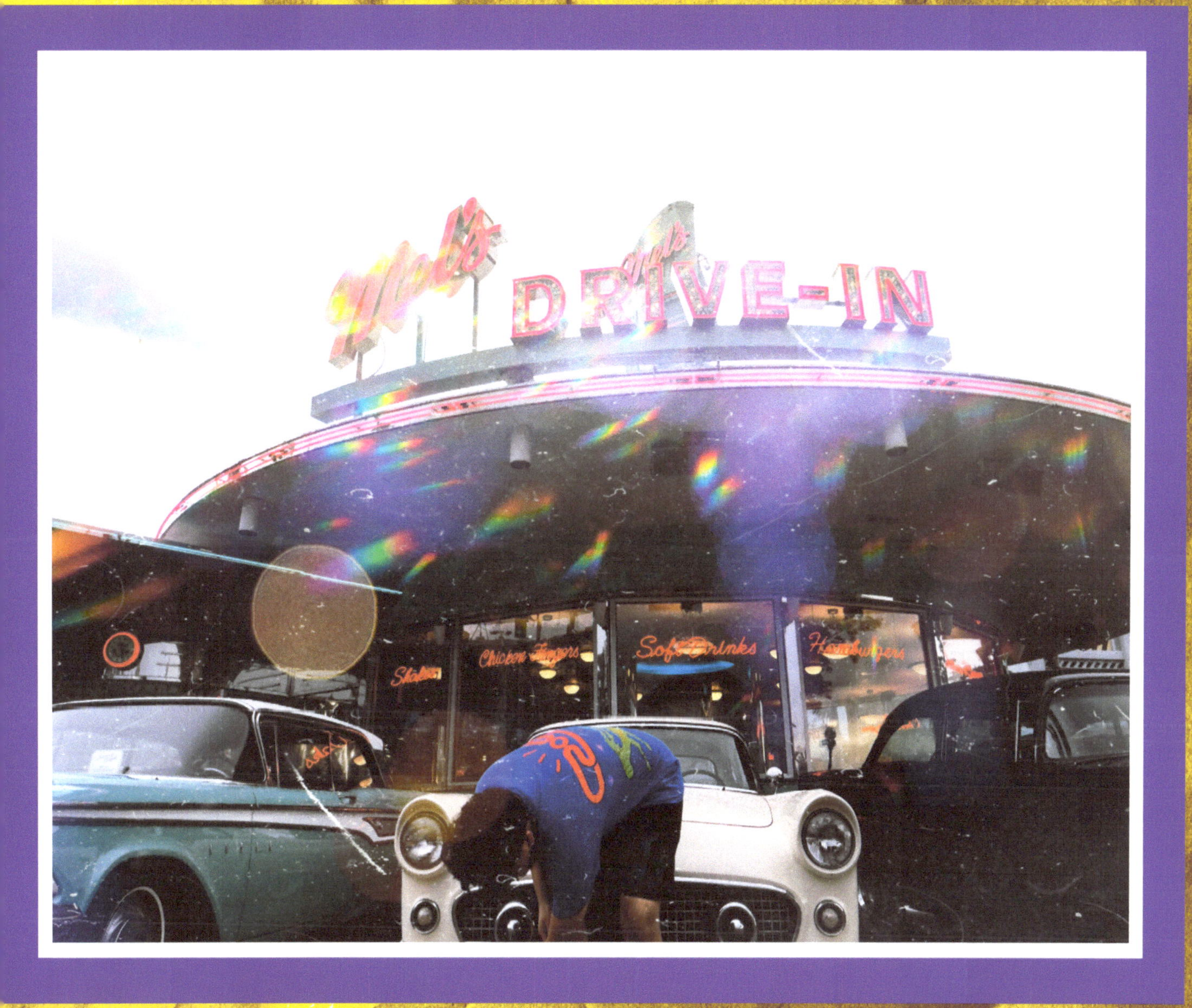

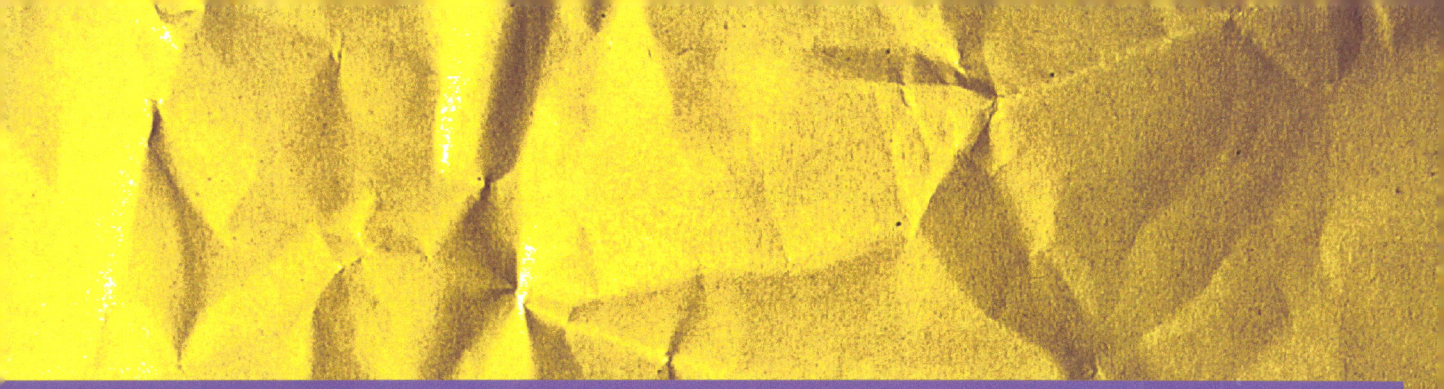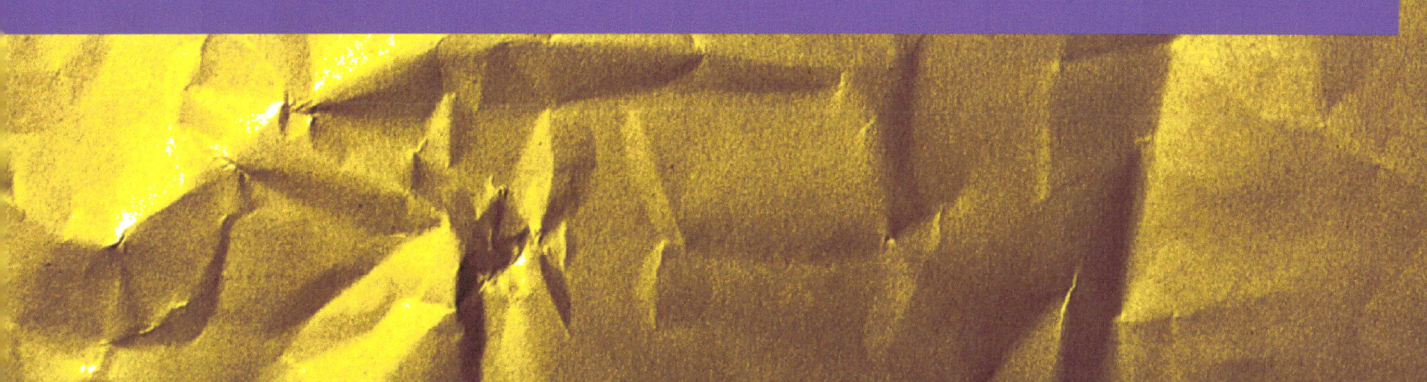

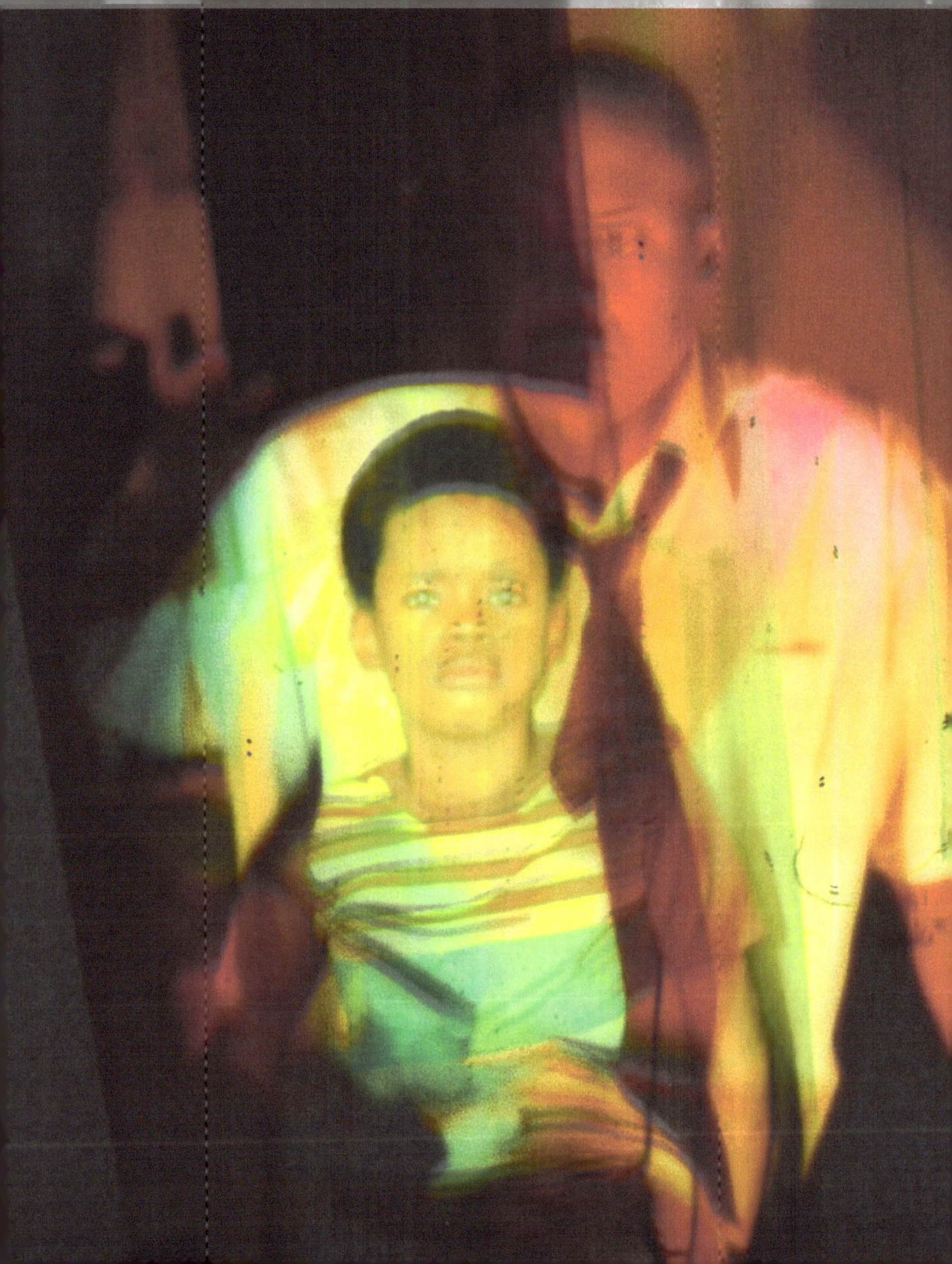

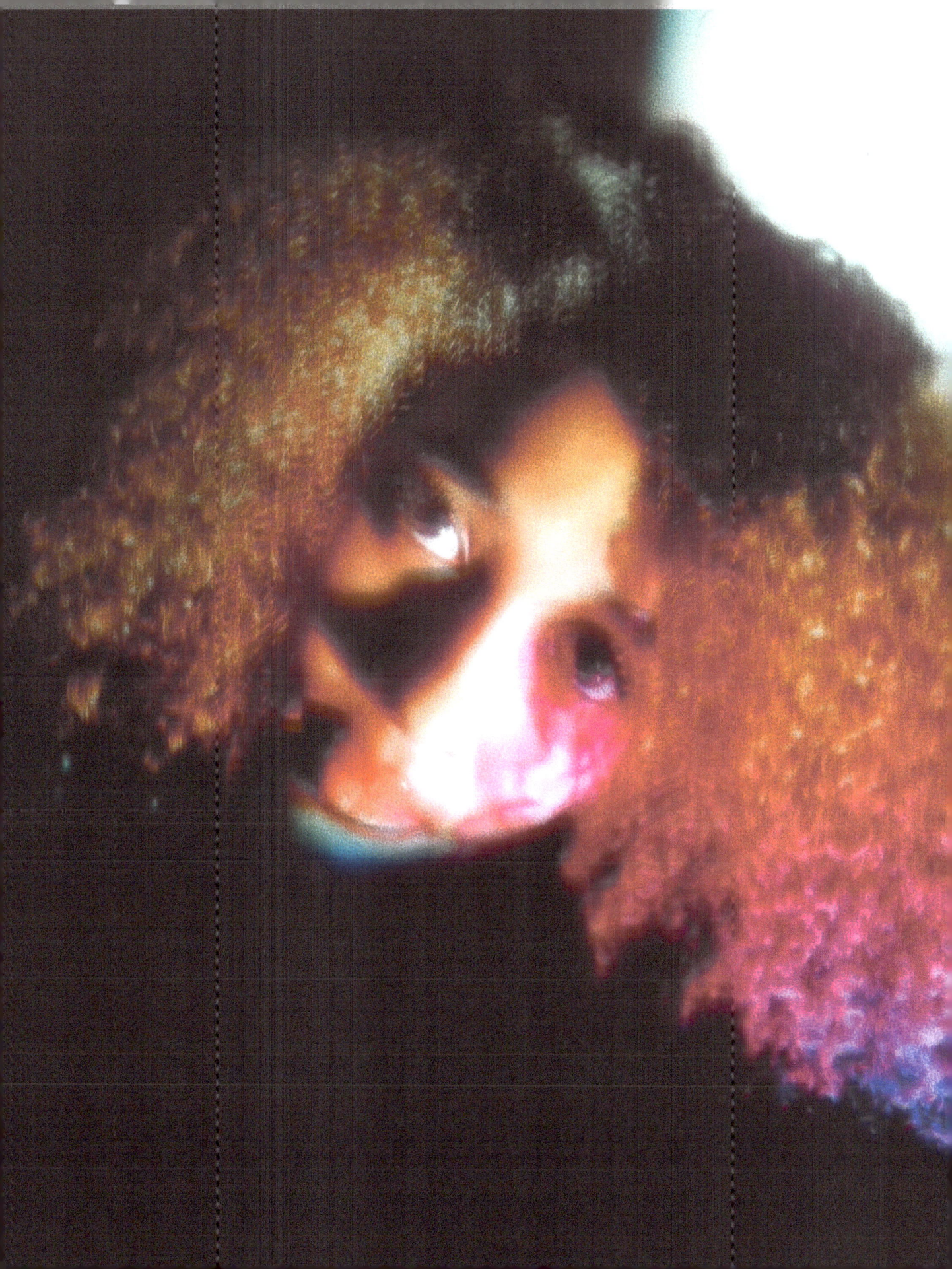

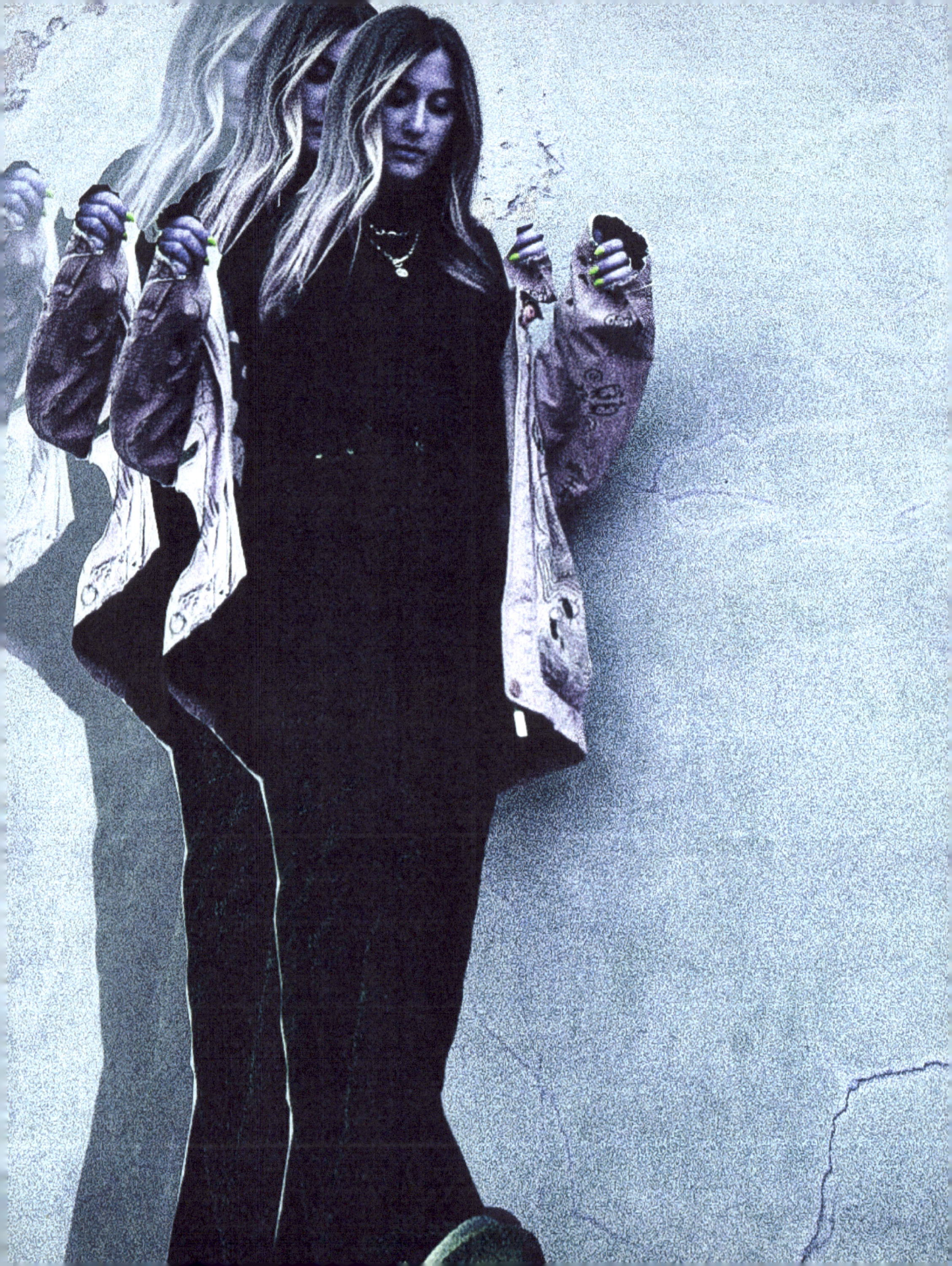

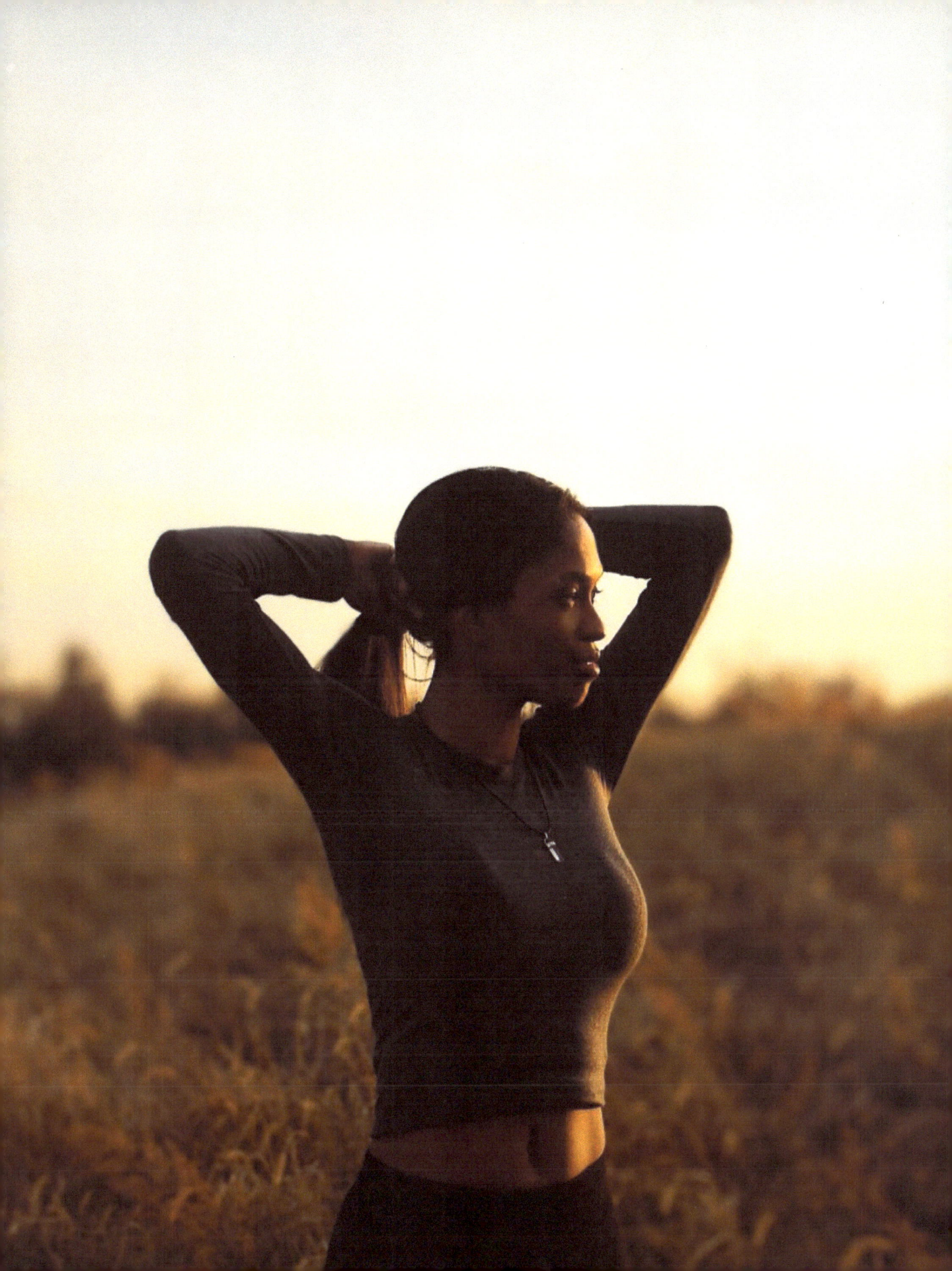

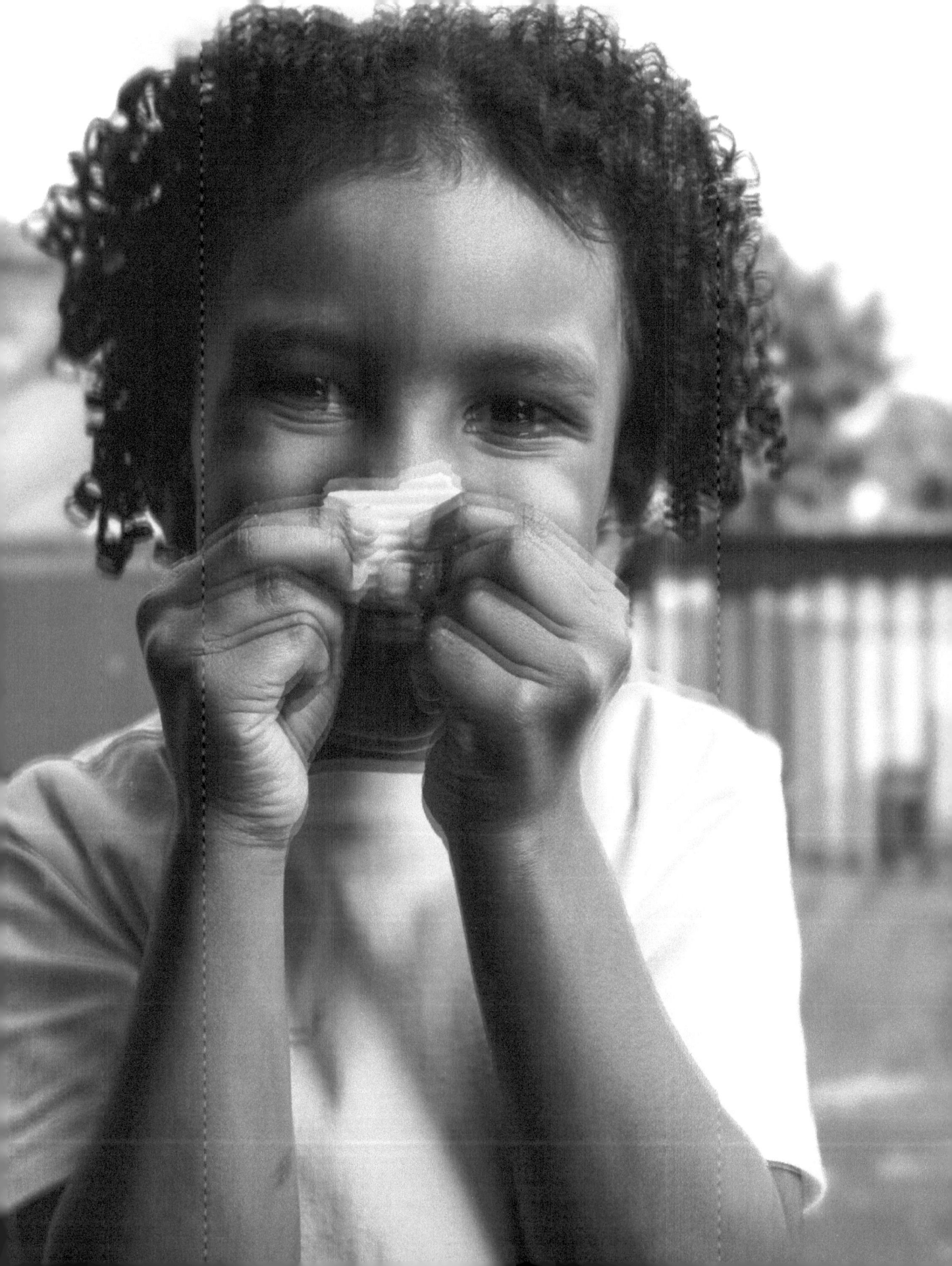

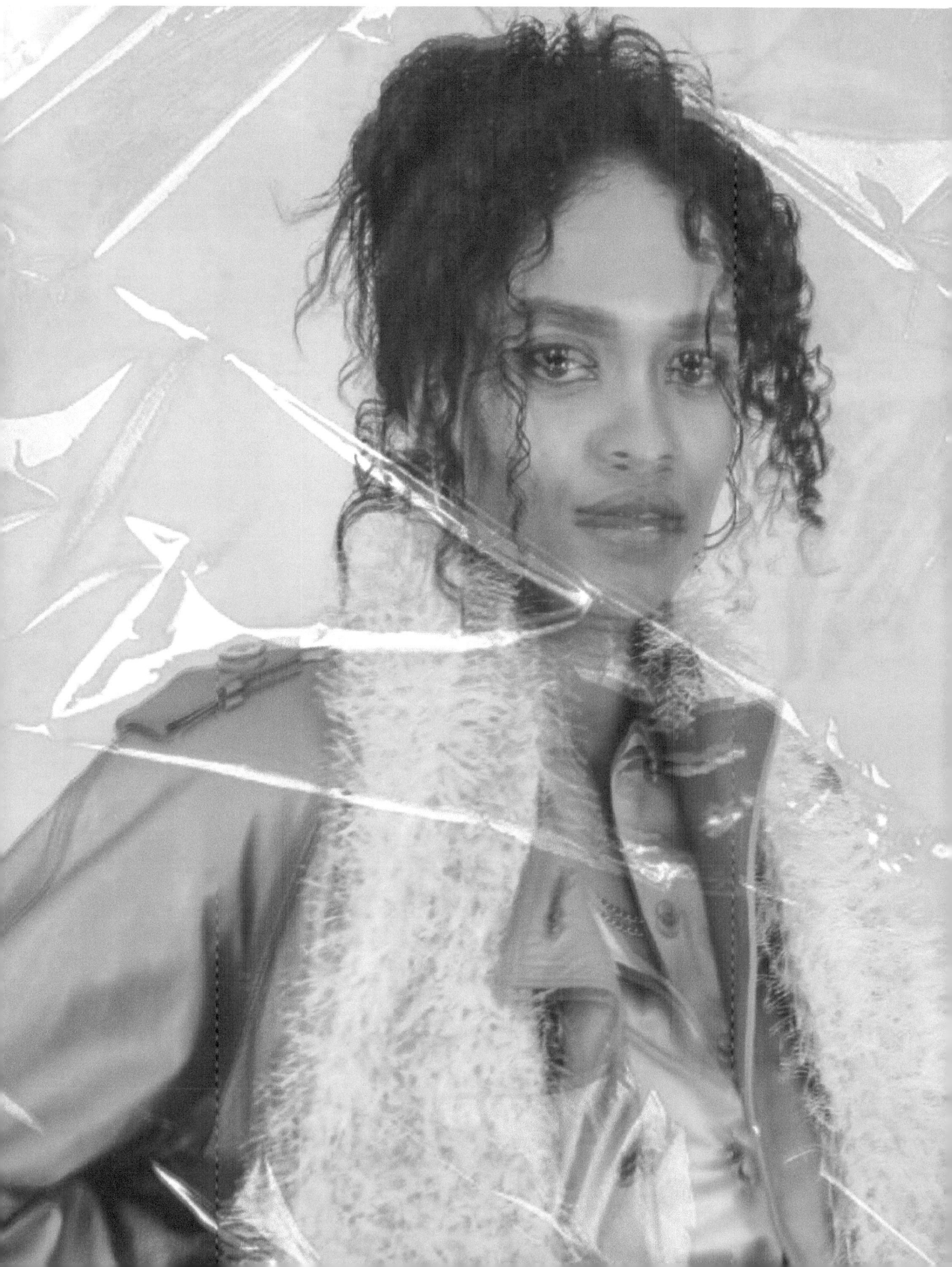

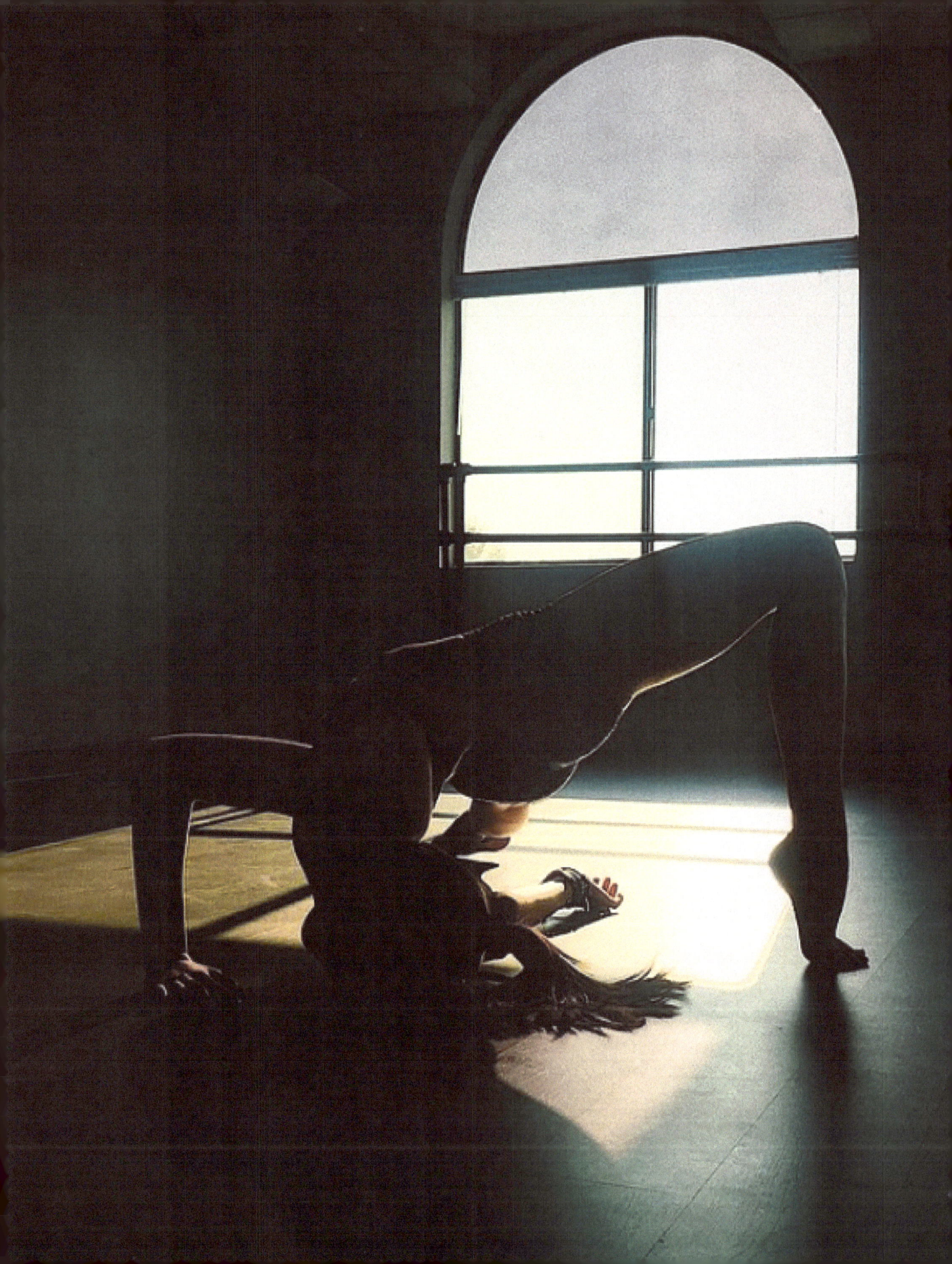

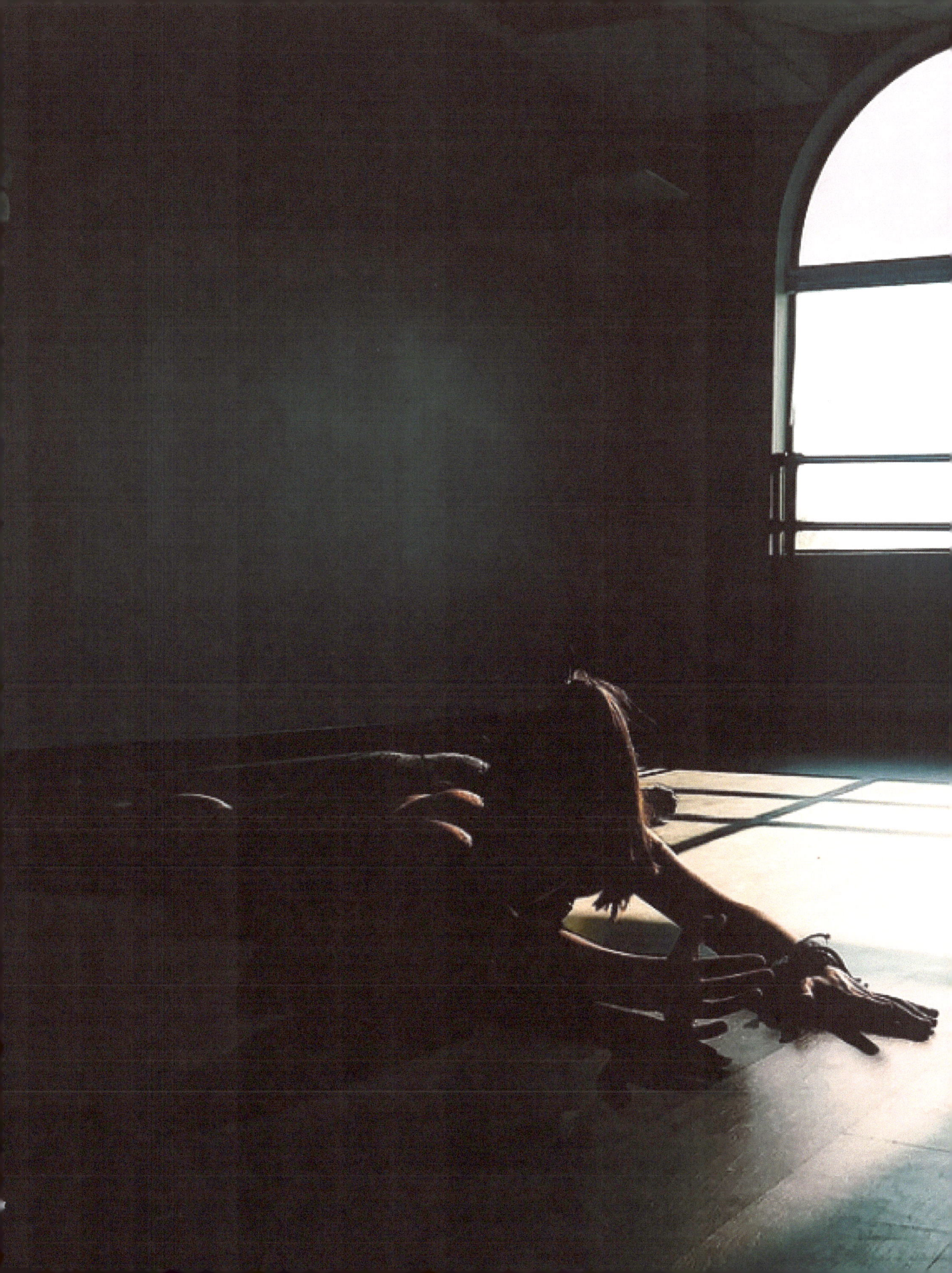